Writing Urban Space

Exploring the relationship
between imaginative writing
and the built environment

Writing Urban Space

Exploring the relationship
between imaginative writing
and the built environment

Edited by Liam Murray Bell
& Gavin Goodwin

Winchester, UK
Washington, USA

First published by Zero Books, 2012
Zero Books is an imprint of John Hunt Publishing Ltd., Laurel House, Station Approach,
Alresford, Hants, SO24 9JH, UK
office1@o-books.net
www.o-books.com

For distributor details and how to order please visit the 'Ordering' section on our website.

Text copyright: Liam Murray Bell and Gavin Goodwin 2011

ISBN: 978 1 78099 254 9

A CIP catalogue record for this book is available from the British Library.

Design: Stuart Davies

Printed and bound by CPI Group (UK) Ltd, Croydon, CR0 4YY

We operate a distinctive and ethical publishing philosophy in all
areas of our business, from our global network of authors to
production and worldwide distribution.

CONTENTS

Introduction

From William Blake through to Iain Sinclair literature has sought to engage with and transform urban space; and, as it is this space in which more and more of us find ourselves living, this engagement has never been more pertinent. This is reflected not only by the growing interest in reading literary texts through the lens of postmodern spatial theories, but also in architects seeking the input of poets and in the employment of storytelling in urban regeneration. This collection of essays seeks to explore this relationship between imaginative writing and the built environment from a variety of perspectives about a variety of places — from London to New Orleans, Copenhagen to Vienna, Northern Ireland to South Wales, Canada to Columbia. Most of the contributors to this collection discuss how this relationship between language and place manifests in their own work (whether that be fiction, poetry, serial plays or site installations), while others interrogate the work of other writers.

The term 'writer' is a flexible concept here. For instance, performance poet Pete Bearder's essay focuses on how mass produced signs and slogans have taken over the urban environment, producing a media-owned space that suffocates the public's right to be heard. His essay contends that these 'meme superhighways' can be subverted through 'small visual or verbal spanners'. Bearder discusses how practices such as graffiti art and billboard liberation are politically radical whether, domestically, highlighting the 'gentrification' of Britain, or, internationally, interrogating politics in South America.

This theme also resonates in Liam Murray Bell's essay on the murals of Northern Ireland. Bell sees these murals functioning as a form of community activism and expression, a space upon which the oppositional politics of Northern Ireland is repre-sented, but also a space for personal catharsis; a creative vent in a time of conflict. In the context of his own fiction, however, the murals further act as territorial signifiers, as important indicators of boundaries and denotations of space that allow him to map the city of Belfast within his novel.

This concern with mapping recurs in Jane Cali-Madell's exploration of Vienna, in which she undergoes a narrative journey through its streets, creating 'images of space and place where before there were none'. Cali-Madell augments this engagement with the city and its history with an exploration of Freudian ideas of the living burial and the desire to return to the womb, as she seeks a greater understanding of the blind protagonist of her novel-in-progress.

Becky Cremin, however, is concerned with disrupting the city and its sign systems. Drawing on the work of Michel de Certeau she employs her serial play as a method of interruption. Building on the ideas of Carla Harryman, Cremin is interested in how performance is part of a '(re)finding and (re)situating' of the body within the city and the establishing of a 'parallelism between the body and the social order.'

Sarah Butler, also using de Certeau's 'practiced place', is interested not with disruption but regeneration. Via 'co-authored stories' her work aims to 'enable people to communicate with architects, planners, and developers, so that they start to feel that they have agency over and responsibility for the places they use', approaching the public's right to be heard from an alternative angle to Bearder. More than this, Butler demonstrates how narrative elements can be incorporated into the very 'physical design' of spaces such as playgrounds, and posits the similarities between building and writing.

This latter issue is further explored by Rosa Ainley, who writes that 'both writing and architecture start by imagining the unimaginable, giving it form'. Ainley's piece centres around one house in particular, and draws on Gaston Bachelard's idea of 'topoanalysis' with its concern with 'the systematic psychological study of the sites of intimate lives'. She discusses her engagement with the 'creating and revealing' of what she calls 'interstitial spaces'. This interest in the liminal, in spaces that 'cross or allow the crossing of borders', links back to Cremin who states: 'it is this BETWEEN which is of interest in performance.'

Like Ainley, Gavin Goodwin's piece focuses on one building (a Brutalist high school in South Wales) and the lives of those that inhabit it. In particular he is interested in examining the gap that often exists between the ideals of the architect and the lived experience of the user, and draws on Lefebvrian ideas of conceived and lived space to explore this in a poetic context. Following the example of George Oppen, Goodwin employs 'found text' within his poem to represent a polyphony of different voices, a technique that is also a central concern of Elizabeth-Jane Burnett's essay on the work of Cynthia Hogue and Rebecca Ross.

Burnett's piece explores how, in the aftermath of Hurricane Katrina, 'documentary reportage', in the form of found materials, interviews and photographs, seemed like the apposite way to react artistically to a humanitarian and environmental tragedy in light of the realisation that the poet can't speak on behalf of the citizens affected. She discusses the difficulty of responding creatively to a natural disaster, a theme that also underpins the last essay in this collection by Jenna Butler. Further, Burnett also discusses the extent to which drawing attention to issues like contaminated milk in Bogota, Columbia – by placing images in an urban space – can become a form of speaking out against political or social injustice, a concept that resonates with Bell's work on the murals of Northern Ireland.

Jan Hatt-Olsen's poetry installations, on the other hand, are less overtly political. Instead they aspire to a Blakean transformation of the city, by literally turning a part of the town of Værløse into a collection of poetry – with pieces of text stuck to the road that people cycling to work can read like scrolls. The end aim of this, for Hatt-Olsen, is to highlight what he sees as the poetry that is already inherent in the urban landscape. His work also connects to Sarah Butler's essay in discussing the idea of writing as socially participatory process.

Holly Prescott is less interested in how space is socially constructed, than with those places that have been abandoned. In her essay she points to what she sees as the shortcomings of the theories of Lefebvre and de Certeau, among others. Prescott argues that in the novels of Nicolas Royle not only does space become a 'catalyst for the narrative itself', but drawing on theories of affect, she suggests that 'disused and redeveloped spaces tak[e] on something of an agency of their own, above and beyond human actualization'.

Including extracts from his novella, David Ashford's piece draws on the late writings of Derrida to investigate the construction of a Gorilla House at London Zoo as a 'blueprint for the future development of the human metropolis'. For Ashford this modernist space that resisted being lived in and the tragic end that met the baby gorillas that were housed there was symptomatic of 'a terrible mistake in Cartesian philosophy underpinning modernist thought'.

Thus, we arrive at Jenna Butler's essay that discusses her attempt to use her poetry to speak to a Canadian natural disaster from 1903, the Frank Slide, engaging with ideas of how we, as a society, have moved away from the natural world and towards 'industrial excess'. Jenna sets her own work in the context of the Mennonite poet Di Brandt, who comes from a simple, rural way of life and attempts to articulate and engage with the urban environment and the 'failed utopia of modernism'. Her discussion of Brandt's struggle to interact echoes, humanises and poeticises the resistance Ashford identifies in the Gorilla House.

The concerns of these essays overlap and interpenetrate, with each serving to enhance, challenge or complicate the other. A writer's engagement with urban space is no more straightforward than her/his engagement with anything else. Thus, whether gaining agency over the streets via storytelling or subverting the media onslaught by interrogating how our perception is constructed or how our bodies form the city; whether the concerns are domestic, political, environmental or spiritual; whether in celebration, condemnation or regeneration; the writing of urban space is considered in this collection as something both complex and urgent.

Word on the Street: Subvertising and Rewriting the Urban Visual Landscape with Street Art

Pete Bearder

Radical street art is about reclaiming the urban environment for an alternative discussion that those in charge would rather we did not have. In modern times, one of the largest targets of radical street art has been to satirise, parody and destroy what has been described as "the largest single psychological project ever undertaken by the human race" - corporate advertising.[1] Radicals say, because the concentration of media ownership has suffocated the public's right to be heard. American Labour Rights Activist Tim Brissell argues that "people resent the destruction of culture and its replacement with these mass produced corporate logos and slogans street artists who seek to reshape the ambient spectacle of the city operate under the belief that media saturation of the urban environment has had a negative impact on public psychological and physical health. This is not all that is at stake. Freedom of speech is under threat, they say. It represents a kind of cultural fascism."[2]

Subvertising

Subvertising is the practice of throwing small visual or verbal spanners into the work of advertising. By making skilful changes to corporate messages it is possible for any pedestrian to spoof, parody and satire the biggest of multinational corporations with a stencil, a poster or the simple stroke of a pen or a spray can. Coca-Cola becomes Killer-Cola, Shell becomes Hell, 'Just Do It' becomes 'Just Screw It' and so on. By hi-jacking their targets, they benefit from the millions of dollars spent on brand recognition and publicity. Subverts can be powerful, apt, rude or funny. Their cheeky nature makes them highly photographic and imitable subjects for discussion.

Kalle Lasn (author and editor of *Adbusters* magazine) describes the process as "uncooling brands", something that "cuts through the hype and the glitz of our mediated reality and momentarily, tantalizingly, reveals the hollow spectacle within".[3] He places this in a larger strategy of "demarketing"; the act of "unselling the consumer society; turning the incredible power of marketing against itself."[4] This is the world of 'culture jamming'. Subverts take their place within this as a form of 'social hacking' or 'meme hacking'.

In the 1990's, ethologist and evolutionary biologist, Richard Dawkins first coined the term 'meme' as a unit of cultural ideas, practices or symbols that (like genes) evolve, mutate and compete for reproductive success. Unlike genes, memes transmit between *minds* rather than through bodies. They reproduce and replicate through writing, speech, rituals, gestures or other imitable cultural phenomena. Urban city centres, then, can be described as meme superhighways. They provide a space where visual representations of conflicting agendas, ideologies and brands evolve and compete at an accelerated pace. As advertising strategies and communication medias develop, memes reproduce with increasing sophistication. A good meme hack will successfully subvert this memetic code and will go viral with the aid of a photograph, an email or word of mouth. Subverts and other forms of radical street art take up arms in what Marshall McLuhan in 1968 predicted would become the Third World War "a guerrilla information war with no division between military and civilian participation"[5].

Potent memes can change minds, alter behaviour, catalyze collective mindshifts and transform cultures. Which is why meme wars have become the geopolitical battleground of our age[6]

Billboard Liberation

Perhaps the most visible way to prick people's consciousness is to deface billboards. The Billboard Liberation Front started in San Francisco in 1977. It was founded on the idea that citizens can, and should, employ their imagination in changing the messages of corporate advertising. Billboards, they say, should be used as a medium for public expression, protest and social communication rather than for private commercialism. They state that their work is not 'illegal' but instead 'un-voicible' within a dominant ideology of consumerism and corporate power.

> Old fashioned notions about art, science and spirituality being the peak achievements and the noblest goals of the spirit of man have been dashed on the crystalline shores of acquisition; the holy pursuit of consumer goods. All old forms and philosophies have been cleverly co-opted and re "spun" as marketing strategies and consumer campaigns by the new shamans, the Ad Men.[7]

In 1990, Reverend Calvin O. Butts of the Abyssinian Baptist Church in Harlem, New York, targeted predatory tobacco and alcohol billboards in poorer black and Hispanic neighbourhoods. He would replace the standard Surgeon General's Warning with: "Struggle General's Warning: Blacks and Latinos are prime scape-goats for illegal drugs, and the prime targets for legal ones."[8] In the 1980s media activists came to Oxford for a billboard blackout competition. After an informal conference about media and alter-native media, participants split up, ran across Oxford, and painted almost all the billboards black.

In 2000 in New York, a group called The Public Ad Campaign organized a guerrilla operation that went one step further in their attempts to reclaim public space. The group (comprising volun-teers and artists), white-washed and redecorated 120 billboards that they identified as being without legal permit. The Public Ad Campaign are part of a large national network of well organized community associations that are working to protect cityscapes and their inhabitants from unwanted advertising and the harmful effects of the 'Ad Men'.

Subvert to the Left?

Do subverts have to be politically radical? Strictly speaking they do not. Subverts are essentially visual puns and can be used by anyone, including political parties or large companies. Overwhelmingly, however, they are associated with anti-corporate or anti-establishment perspectives. One of the central purposes of subvertising (called ad-busting in the U.S) is to shock the viewer by juxtaposing easily recognisable images with shocking and disturbingly frank realities. Models that appear on posters for the fashion industry have, on countless occasions, had their faces turned skeletal in an effort to highlight the role of such companies in bringing about eating disorders among women. In Oxford, 2008, a billboard for the new BMW Mini was engulfed in pasted-on waves alongside a message about climate change. By encouraging critical thinking in this way, subvertisers seek to challenge received 'wisdom' and to bring about change.

In the UK, one of the most common subject matters for political street art is 'gentrification'. The unregulated and unopposed arrival of private interests to spaces known for their inclusive, diverse or public nature leads to small businesses and poorer inhabitants being priced out of a community. One Oxford based stencil artist developed a series of subverts designed to raise awareness about changes to the Cowley Road area. The Cowley Road, once known for its radical politics and under-ground music scene, has been heavily sanitised by the arrival of chain stores, students and an increased police presence. Carefully targeted and strategically placed subverts transform Costa Coffee into Costly Coffee, Subway into Sadway and

Subvert, Tesco into Tescopoly and Blockbuster into Blockbusted.

Street artist Erik Triantafillou, however, believes that such pieces are limited in scope. They are not, for example, able to give the viewer a deeper understanding of gentrification's complex 'socio-historical dynamic'. Instead they deal in 'binary idioms' that fail to encompass the rainbow of social actors involved: from banks, planners and developers through to property owners, exploited construction workers and community associations.

> the image of colonising yuppies in search of authentic cultural interaction flattens this complex set of actors and interests into an easy-to-digest call to action...the spatial component of capitalism's necessity to continuously accumulate and expand – is something these symbols cannot communicate, and in fact obfuscate.[9]

The picture becomes even more confused when we look at some unlikely reactions to the work of the best known of all radical street artists – Banksy. In April 2009 an anti–police piece of his was defaced in Bristol. A group called Appropriate Media claimed responsibility, stating that "graffiti artists are the performing spray-can monkeys for gentrification"[10]. This incident represents one of the more militant examples of growing opposition to such art work on the grounds that it makes the area more desirable to property speculators. This means increased rents and displaced poor.

In 1998, under the Serbian dictatorship of Milosevic, we see an example of 'official' and 'un-official' street art blurring. Otpor (meaning 'Resistance' in Serb), was a student network that opposed Milosevic. They received a donation of over one million pounds from George Sorros. Most of this was spent on spray-paint and stickers to plaster the country with anti-Milosevic street art. They helped to overthrow the dictator later that year.[11] George Sorros is a Hungarian-American currency speculator, stock investor, businessman, philanthropist, and political activist. His CV does not fit neatly with the usual stereotype of how street art is generated.

In Caracas, Venezuela, we can find another unusual case study. The graffiti writing group Guerrilla Communications is a project of the Ministry of Communes; a branch of the revolutionary government of Hugo Chavez. It offers graffiti and stencil workshops around the city in an effort to 'communicate the revolution'. Others (like the Communications Liberation Army) have more independence, but still get material like spray paint from the government. This is state sponsored propaganda with a difference. According to Sujatha Fernandes, a sociologist at Queens College in New York:

> These groups share the objective of reclaiming public space and turning it into a kind of street periodical that can be constantly renewed and painted over to get their message out.[12]

In neighbouring Colombia, where politics is very much a matter of life and death, the remaining public universities provide concrete canvasses for political discourse. As well as idolising leftist war heroes, factions and ideologies, the pieces communicate a huge array of political issues that are marginalised from the mainstream media: police assassination of student activists, university privatisation and opposition to international trade agreements and US imperialism.

Similarly, in New York, marginalised communities paint street memorials for departed community members. These serve as road side shrines, turning public spaces into sites of collective memory. Pieces such as these represent what Jeff Ferrell describes as a 'visual conversation'. It is necessary, he claims, because ""public" officials have disallowed murals dealing with police brutality, war, AIDS, and other topics".[13]

Tools of the Trade

In the last 2 decades, culture jamming has gone high tech – with computer programmes such as Photoshop enabling people to match fonts, colours and materials more precisely. Simultaneously there has been the rise of culture jammers that colonise cyperscapes with their words and images and 'hacktivists' that infiltrate and subvert corporate websites.[14]

But it need not be any more high tech than a permanent marker. For poster street artists, the medium is paper, print and wallpaper paste. For them, the low-tech nature of artisan street art is central to encouraging participation. It stands in contrast to mass produced art that is geared towards maximum exposure, maximum coverage and maximum output. "It is important to be reminded to slow down" says poster artist Sam Sebren. "Making and seeing handmade art are poetic, necessary reminders of human energy and personal and political expression".[15]

Fellow artist Claude Moller describes this as "a good example of unalienated labor". In an almost communist analysis, he claims that the art becomes empowering when "control of production" is "in the hands of the creators".[16] Political print maker Dylan Miner agrees, claiming that the scale of street art, the materials it uses and the spaces in which it is seen make it an "accessible and non-elitist" art form. Poster prints are a practical and accessible way of circulating material amongst large audiences without it "being contained with capitalist social relations".[17]

The Role of the Artist

Ad busting is a tool for artists to take a proactive approach to commercial infringements on public space. The role of the artist is transformed and put towards a direct community service, rather than serving a commercial agenda for the sake of a salary. In the words of Erik Triantafillou, it creates "spaces for collective reflection and political education."[18] Media activist Emily Pohl

Weary describes this as nothing less than "an evolving medium of social dissent, community communication and grassroots promotion"[19]. These posters enable independent artists to interact directly with people in their community.

It changes the perception of urban space into something that is shaped and improved by the people who live there, and turns skyscrapers and concrete into a home that visitors quickly identify as a unique and individual community.[20]

Conclusion

The streets of the modern city provide a visual battleground for public consciousness. Subverts are effective when they succeed in planting a seed in the viewer's mind. For the converted, the artwork will be empowering because it alerts them to the presence of others who hold a given belief or viewpoint and are prepared to break the law to express it.

With some notable exceptions, it is a direct and unmediated art form. Nothing comes between the pedestrian and the artist who remains independent of large scale finance. By design, it sets itself apart from the commercial agenda of advertising. This is significant because it is about where, why and by whom the words and images that convey our culture are conceived.

Moreover, it helps shape identity and gives a voice to sidelined communities and marginalized viewpoints, be they geographically sidelined, stigmatized as criminals or simply frustrated. Artists are able to combat the pollution of our urban visual landscape by profit-driven enterprises that are becoming increasingly sophisticated at catching our eyes and arousing our desires at every street corner. Though it is mostly illegal it is the product of citizens reasserting their right to artistic and political expression and their sovereignty over public space.

Bibliography

Kalle Lasn, *Culture Jam: How to Reverse America's Suicidal Customer Binge – and Why We Must* (London: HarperCollins, 2000)

Naomi Klein, *No Logo* (London: Flamingo, 2001)

Dylan Mathews, *War Prevention Works: 50 Stories of People Resolving Conflict,* (London: Oxford Research Group, 2001)

Marshall McLuhan, *Culture is Our Business,* (New York: Ballantine Books, 1970)

Jeff Ferrell, *Tearing Down the Streets: Adventures in Urban Anarchy,* (London: Palgrave MacMillan, 2001)

Paper Politics by Josh McPhee (Oakland, California: PM Press, 2010)

Websites

www.bilboardliberation.org

www.nytimes.com

www.bbc.co.uk

http://colombiasolidarity.blogspot.com/2007/07/grafitti-in-universidad-nacional-bogota.html

www.hackcanada.com

http://www.adbusters.org/

http://www.graffiti.org/ - AKA 'Artcrimes'

http://woostercollective.com/

http://urbanprankster.com/

Writing on the Walls: Discourses of Violence and Catharsis in the Murals of Northern Ireland

Liam Murray Bell

We begin with a disclaimer: this essay is not intended as a chronology of mural-painting in Belfast and Derry, nor is it presumed to be an exhaustive study of the symbolic value of the murals. Such discussions of historical significance and the potential for murals to function as iconography can be found elsewhere[21]. Instead, this essay deals with the possibility for the imaginative integration of the murals into writings about the North of Ireland. That is, it is concerned with the ways that murals may manifest themselves in contemporary literature and the prospective value of them for writers— such as myself— who deal with the period of the Troubles. In order to do this, a three-strand approach will be adopted. First of all, I will examine murals as providing an expression for collective feeling, focusing on the extent to which murals represent the communities whose gable walls they occupy, and the degree to which graffiti can perform a similar function. Then I will discuss the possibility of articulating the personal through the mural in a cathartic way; the opportunity for utilising this urban canvas as a creative vent in a time of conflict. Finally, the essay will address the importance of murals as territorial signifiers; essentially as signposts marking out the oppositional communities. These three sections will be related to my novel entitled *So It Is*, which details the discourses of violence that the protagonist, Aoife, appropriates in the wake of the maiming of her brother, Damien, at the hands of the British Security Services.

* * *

It can be argued that the tradition of mural painting has been maintained as it provides a method for the communities of Northern Ireland to represent themselves and to communicate their beliefs and political opinions to both their own support-base and then on out into the wider world. Alex Maskey, the former Sinn Féin Mayor of Belfast, has noted that the murals "echo the feelings of the majority of the people"[22] in any given area, and Tim Pat Coogan states that "mural culture has traditionally expressed the strident emotions of the Six County streets"[23]. Yet it is telling that the majority of murals express some affiliation with a paramilitary grouping and it is difficult, therefore, to determine whether it is fear of reprisal or, instead, organic and quantifiable popular support that sustains them. There are over five-hundred murals documented in the University of Ulster's CAIN database[24] and these compiled images only account for roughly a quarter of the murals that have been painted since the onset of the Troubles in 1969, without even accounting for those that have been repainted or significantly changed as the conflict has progressed. It is true to say that they are the images most associated with Northern Ireland, with many news presenters and documentary makers featuring them in their programmes. (An episode of Channel 4's *Come Dine With Me*[25] featured stills of the murals to establish that the programme was set in Belfast, even though such images obviously bear no relevance to the show's content). Murals have, of course, also made appearances in the fiction produced from Northern Ireland, with Robert McLiam Wilson, for example, talking of them in his novel *Eureka Street* by writing: "The city keeps its walls like a diary. In this staccato shorthand, the walls tell of histories and hatred, shrivelled and bleached with age."[26] However, it is debatable whether these symbols of conflict truly represent the two traditions of Northern Ireland— which can be categorised as Nationalist and Unionist— or just the two often-violent factions— which can be categorised as Republican and Loyalist.

Loyalist murals tend to characterised by staunch defiance, by military imagism and by statements that assert the Unionist right to remain as part of the United Kingdom. Often the images and messages convey the Unionist community as maintaining an historical affinity with either the British Empire or with Protestant culture. For instance, many murals depict King William of Orange at the Battle of the Boyne on 1st July 1690, or commemorate the Battle of the Somme— which began on the same date in 1916— in which many Ulstermen lost their lives fighting for Britain. In a similar way, Republican murals often attempt to trace a lineage back through significant events in the history of the Republicanism in Ireland. Therefore, it is common to see images of the H-Block hunger-strikers of 1981, such as Bobby Sands (see Figure 1); slogans or images relating to events on Bloody Sunday in Derry, 30th January 1972; or even representations of Irish mythology, through paintings of figures such as the warrior Cúchulainn. As Robin Morgan has noted "the Provisional IRA wage battle in order to carry on the work of their political and literal (martyred) fathers"[27], so the mural for the Republican community becomes about tracing a history of struggle and contextualising their own violence in relation to the conflict that has preceded it. In short, the mural operates as a means of politicizing the violence. This is not to say that all Loyalist murals have an aspect of militarism, or indeed that no Republican murals portray the strength of the groupings such as the PIRA. I wanted to detail the types of murals produced by the two communities, though, to highlight the difference between murals– by which I mean a tradition of painstakingly produced images and representations, often aligned with paramilitary groupings, that occupy the walls and gable-ends of houses in the communities that, by-and-large, support their actions— and simple graffiti.

Figure 1: Mural of Bobby Sands on the gable wall of the Sinn Féin
offices. Falls Road, Belfast. Image by Conor Edgell.

Graffiti implies a lack of legitimacy, in terms of being represen-
tative, because of its amateur appearance. To cite an example, a
wall in the South of Belfast which bears the words, 'Ulster Says
No to the Politicans', can— quite apart from the misspelling of
'politicians'— be seen as amateur, in comparison with the
murals, due to the fading paint and irregular lettering. Or,
occasionally, graffiti in Belfast can be seen to be necessarily
opportune. For instance, the message 'collusion starts here'
sprayed on the outside of a heavily-fortified police barracks has
been scrawled there hurriedly due to an inability, on the part of
the artist, to camp outside the barracks and lovingly paint a
mural. Whatever the scenario, however, murals are seen as being
reasonable and justifiable expressions of community in a time of
conflict— or, as Neil Jarman states, "as an established, if not
entirely legitimate, political practice"[28]— whereas graffiti is
viewed as being anti-social, loutish and certainly not represen-
tative of the community.

This is a distinction which I have been keen to explore in my writing, with the main character of Aoife reflecting on these differing perceptions in a passage during which her own resentment is growing:

Reaching for the remote, Aoife turned up the volume on the telly in the corner. The reporter, speaking over the top of a series of images, was on about graffiti and how the intricate artistic detail of the murals was being lost to scrawled words of Sectarian hatred. Aoife would have put money on it, though, that the worry wasn't about the hate – they were more worried about losing those American tourists who had started going on bus tours around the murals. It had been a growth industry since the ceasefire, the so-called terror tours. And the Americans weren't wanting to see misspelt declarations from dissident republicans that related to what was happening in the here-and-now, they were wanting to see lovingly painted gunmen and shrines to martyrs who'd died back in the days when their parents had first left the old country.

The picture on the telly cut to a picture of a shuttered shop that had 'The war is not over' spray-painted across the front of it in awkward spidery letters. Probably written by the Continuity IRA or a lone vandal, the reporter speculated. Aoife smiled softly to herself. It did her head in how the media had this attitude that the murals were somehow the only representation of community feeling, whilst some wee spide spray-painting 'Brits out' on a garden wall was just to be ignored. The difference between the murals and graffiti wasn't that one was a collective expression of feeling and the other was just some hallion acting out, it was that people would pay to see the murals but if they just wanted graffiti or anything like that there then they could see it in whichever town or city they'd sprung from. Belfast was the same as any other city, people wrote on the walls because that was where they knew it'd be seen.

This passage, you may have noticed, also references the increased commerciality and global-appeal of the murals as tourist attractions. Buses and black taxis will now take tourists on so-called 'terror tours' of Belfast and this is seen as a way of gaining an insight into the psyche of the people of the city. The danger of affording the murals this significance, however, as indicators of public opinion— as I seek to address through Aoife's narrative— is that they tend to be generalised views, collectivised views and, such is the manner of their sponsorship by paramilitary organisations, often views that may not adequately express the opinions of the people who live in that area or community. To put it another way, to scrawl graffiti on a wall you require only a tin of spray-paint, but to paint a mural you require the support of local politicians, community workers, residents and— often most importantly— the boys in balaclavas.

* * *

Which brings me to murals and graffiti as a personal and cathartic expression of resentment engendered by perceived occupation or politicized violence. Depictions of Belfast during the Troubles, both through the murals and through other modes, tend to focus on the bleak, the violent and the relentlessly negative. Yet there are, in a contemporary context, examples of murals that are expressive and creative and which function as art as much as they function as symbols. In his Nobel Prize Speech in 1995 the Northern poet Seamus Heaney noted: "I began a few years ago to try to make space in my reckoning and imagining for the marvellous as well as for the murderous"[29]. He is referring to the cultivation of a gap within the conflict in which artists can express themselves, through whichever mode is available to them. Thus, members of the community can utilise the public forum of gable-ends and communal walls to articulate their own feelings towards the undulating violence of the Troubles.

It is a challenge which has been taken up by one group in particular, the Bogside Artists in Derry. Their mission statement includes a passage which sums up their cathartic response to their artworks: "Our fervent wish is that the peace process will give us time to put right what has been so drastically put wrong. To this end we devote our craft and our energy, our imagination, our story and our hope."[30] The almost revolutionary zeal of this statement shows the potential for murals to function as a salve, healing the wounds of the violence through personal expression and creative endeavour.

This idea, essentially of creative venting, is something that I was keen to explore in my novel through the character of Damien— Aoife's brother who has been maimed by the British Security Forces. This passage details his teenage angst and anger and the gradual fruition of playing the guitar and writing songs as a means of expressing his emotions:

It didn't take long before the writing started. Scrawled lyrics, normally only two or three lines at a time, as fractured and unconnected as his chords, would be noted down on the edges of newspaper columns, the fly-leaves of school books, the block-border of posters, wherever there was blank white space. Damien would write them all down, the procedure requiring not only his tongue to be hanging out of his mouth, but his teeth to clamp it in place as well. Once he'd got his thought down, however short it was, he'd tear the corner of paper – from the newspaper, from the school book, once even from the bog-roll – and add it to the rest of the pile. A tiny mound of over-sized confetti became a hillock, became a hill, became a mountain, became a mountain-range. The paper would drift and then settle in the draft from a door opening-

and-closing, so that the peaks of it were always changing and ever-spreading across the bedroom. Above each lyric would be a chord, a D or an E or a G, that was to be played as the words were soundlessly mouthed, but it would've been near enough impossible to have scooped up a handful of the scraps and come up with anything even close to a song. It would've been like flicking the dial constantly through the radio stations and catching only snippet after unrelated snippet.

The character of Damien goes through this phase of writing down his lyrics on scraps of paper but, as I have hopefully conveyed in the prose, it is an imperfect and impermanent solution. In Northern Ireland a written expression goes onto a wall, is formed as a mural rather than as a discarded note. So, later in the narrative, Damien graduates to writing the lyrics directly onto his bedroom wall:

Like an enormous crossword puzzle, it was, except that if you looked closely no word ever cut across or shared a letter with another. As he went, Damien scrunched his pieces of paper into tight wee balls and dropped them out of the opened window. The mountain-range became a mountain, became a hill, became a hillock. Then even the hillock disappeared, to be scattered like hailstones across the soil of the barren flowerbed beneath his window.

To Aoife's eyes, the assortment of collected words running across the wall looked beautiful. After the black marker had run to grey, Damien picked up the next pen that came to hand, which happened to be blue. Then red, then a slightly deeper shade of blue, then black again. The different colours formed a patchwork that reminded Aoife of all the leaves that used to gather along the pavements up the Malone Road, piles of leaves she'd cycled through when she was younger. Different shades all overlapping, each separate from the next, but each connected somehow. She'd told Joanne about it, one day at school, and Joanne had grandly announced that it was called a mosaic or a montage, depending on whether it was about the different colours that he'd used or the various clutches of words. She had a cousin who was an artist, did Joanne. She seemed to have one relation or another who did near enough everything. All Aoife knew about the writing on the wall was that it filled her with the same joy she'd felt when she used to look out of the window to see the first falling leaf of Autumn spiralling down towards the ground.

In this way the character of Damien appropriates the practice of writing on walls, adopted from the graffiti-scrawlers and mural-painters of the city— in order to afford permanence to his lyrics and to express his emotions in the aftermath of sustaining his injuries— in a similar way to the Bogside Artists, who have taken over a tradition that has tended to produce declarations of war and statements of paramilitary intent and who instead utilise the urban spaces of gable-ends and walls as canvasses.

* * *

The murals have another usage, however, one that is functional and which affords no particular significance to the artwork itself but rather focuses on the importance of location. Allen Feldman in his excellent anthropological study of Belfast, *Formations of Violence*, talks of the city as comprising several inter-connected areas that are formed upon a structure of sanctuary to interface to adversary. That is, he argues that each community has areas that are considered safe- "the sanctuary"- areas that come into contact with the other community- "the interface"- and areas that are considered as 'belonging' to the other community- "the adversary"[31]. Obviously the sanctuary area of one grouping is the adversary area of the other, and vice versa.

This gives rise to another reading of murals, a darker reading that, nonetheless, should certainly be afforded credence. The murals, both in terms of positioning and in terms of the message they convey, denote boundaries. They function as warnings to the other oppositional community to stay away. They are, in essence, enormous 'Stay out' signs, often deviating to notices that are akin to 'Beware of the dog' due to the presence of masked gunmen on the mural. There is an implied threat and warning to their positioning at the edges of the community— whether it is Loyalist or Republican. To cite a couple of examples, the famous mural at what has come to be known as 'Free Derry Corner' is associated with the Battle of the Bogside in 1969[32]. It functions as a statement of community that removes it from its imposed status as an area of the United Kingdom. In essence it is a declaration of independence for the area of the Bogside, an assertion of autonomy— from the rule of the Province's forces of law and order— for the nationalist community that lies beyond. In a similar way, the gable-end that you come across as you drive down Sandy Row in the South of the city functions as an indicator of place by asserting military prowess and affiliation with the notion of an Ulster aligned with the British State (see Figure 2). It is a Loyalist mural—painted in response to Free Derry Corner— that is intended to discourage Republican encroachment into the area and, at the same time, to assure those who live in Sandy Row of their location within a geographical 'sanctuary' zone.

These geographical signposts within the city are useful to myself, as a writer, in that they allow for a clear definition as to when the paramilitary character is safely ensconced within her own community and when she has transgressed the boundaries and is operating in what is essentially enemy territory. This final extract from the novel details this character picking up a potential victim, named Whitey, from within a Loyalist area and bringing

Figure 2: Loyalist Mural. Sandy Row, Belfast.
Image by Conor Edgell.

him back to the sanctuary-zone of the Republican Falls Road. It deals with sexualised violence and her wish to, in essence, kidnap Whitey in order to inflict bodily harm in an act of vengeance:

Whitey is stocious by the time we leave the Regal. Absolutely full. That's how I need them, though, so I've no complaints. I lead him down Conway Street. Past the UVF mural with two sub-machine-

gun wielding paramilitaries guarding plundered poetry written in black and gold: Sneak home and pray you'll never know, The hell where youth and laughter go. *Bleak. He follows me on down Fifth Street, not noticing that we've turned right and right again, not noticing that the flags on the tops of the lampposts are changing. Out onto the Falls Road. We've skirted right around the corrugated peaceline. Whitey seems happy enough, though. Like a dog following a scent, his eyes on me, his hands grabbing for me and, for the most part, missing. Leading him on, past the garden of remembrance. More words in black and gold, but no poetry to them. Lists of the Republican dead.*

Whitey stops under the first mural of the Hunger Strikers and mumbles to himself. As though he's trying to memorise the quote painted on it. Unlikely he'll remember much of anything from the walk home. He'll remember the rest of the night, mind. Pain sobers you up fairly quickly. I steer him to the right before the second mural, the one of Bobby Sands MP. Down Sevastopol Street, then Odessa. Doubling back on myself. It was Baldy who set me up with the place. A safe house. Number 48. The house beside has woodchip across the windows, fly-posters plastered on the woodchip and weeds sprouting from the posters. I check the other side, Number 50. All the lights are out. I don't want there to be kids in next door when Whitey sets to squealing. That sort of thing can leave a kid shook for life.

In this extract, the precursor to the explicit violence that the character enacts upon her drunken victim, we see her leading Whitey away from his own sanctuary space— the border of which is given by the UVF mural— across the interface that is denoted by the corrugated peaceline— constructed by the British to keep the two communities apart— and then on to the Falls Road past the Garden of Remembrance— which lists the names of the Republican dead, many of them IRA volunteers— and then on into what, for Whitey, is an adversary area. The murals in this extract function as territorial signifiers, telling both character and reader where they are geographically. More importantly, however, in a city rife with paramilitary murder and sectarian violence, they also indicate how safe they are and to what extent they can consider themselves within a sanctuary-space.

* * *

As I have examined, then, murals perform an important function within my own writings about Belfast in three different ways: as representations of community feeling, both in the form of murals and as graffiti; as a method of expressing the personal hurt of the Troubles in a cathartic way; and, finally, as affording a series of territorial signifiers that situate both character and reader within the divided landscape of Belfast. Many of the themes evoked by the murals intersect with the narrative of *So It Is*, as the conflict-torn urban space of Belfast impacts upon the characters and as— in turn— the characters seek to impact upon the prevalent discourses of the conflict and attempt to open up an imaginative space into which they can vent, whether that be through the positive of catharsis or through the negative of appropriating violence as a means of releasing their frustration, resentment and anger.

So It Is will be available from Myriad Editions, June 2012: www.myriadeditions.com

Bibliography:

Allen Feldman, *Formations of Violence: The Narrative of the Body and Political Terror in Northern Ireland*, (Chicago and London: The University of Chicago Press, 1991)

Seamus Heaney, *Opened Ground: Poems 1966-1996*, (London: Faber and Faber, 1998)

Tim Pat Coogan, *The Troubles: Ireland's Ordeal 1966-1996 and the*

Search for Peace, (London: Arrow Books, 1996)

Robert McLiam Wilson, *Eureka Street*, (London: Vintage Books, 1998)

Robin Morgan, *The Demon Lover: On the Sexuality of terrorism*, (London: Mandarin, 1990)

Northern Ireland: A Chronology of the Troubles 1968-1993, Paul Bew and Gordon Gillespie (eds), (Dublin: Gill & Macmillan Ltd, 1993)

Symbols in Northern Ireland, Anthony Buckley (ed), (Belfast: The Institute of Irish Studies, 1998)

Neil Jarman, 'Troubled images: the iconography of loyalism' *Critique of Anthropology 12*, (1992) pp.133-45

Bill Rolston, *Drawing support: murals in the North of Ireland* (Belfast: Beyond the Pale Publications, 1992)

Bill Rolston, *Drawing support 2: murals of war and peace*, (Belfast: Beyond the Pale Publications, 1995)

Conflict Archive on the Internet at the University of Ulster (CAIN Database): http://cain.ulst.ac.uk/mccormick/index .html

Website of the Bogside Artists, Derry: http://www.bogsideartists .com/

Come Dine with Me- Belfast: Series 3, Episode 9, Granada Productions for Channel 4, first broadcast on 3rd August 2006

All images provided courtesy of Conor Edgell: conoredgellart .blogspot.com

Mansions of the Mind: Vienna and the Spatial Uncanny

Jane Cali-Madell

When learning the craft of writing, the new writer is frequently exhorted to draw on all five senses: touch, taste, smell, sound and sight. However, as I work on my novel-in-progress, this isn't always possible, since my first person narrator, the eighteenth-century Viennese pianist, Marie-Thérèse von Paradis, is blind. Normally, spatial perception situates the subject clearly in space, and in opposition to it. However, my narrator's spatial awareness is entirely governed by darkness, and therefore by the projections of her own mind. However, on my recent research trip to Vienna, the subject of this essay, I realised that we all interpret the world according to our own mental processes and projections.

Such an awareness has obviously informed the work of many writers. For this essay, it will be considered in relation to my own developing novel— working title, *The Glass Marionette*— and to the writings of Rilke and Hoffmann, as well as to those of the Viennese writers, Musil, Faschinger, and of course, Freud. In particular, aspects of the Freudian uncanny which seem to have a corresponding spatiality, such as the return of the repressed, the fear of burial alive, and the impossible desire to return to the womb will be discussed in terms of my own experiences of Vienna. This is because the January journey that I made through the city, searching for signs of Marie-Thérèse, seemed to me to trace a trajectory analogous to the Freudian uncanny.

This essay will also, therefore, be structured by the journey that I made, and by the places that I visited: the House of Music, Schönbrunn Palace, Doctor Mesmer's mansion and the graveyard of Sankt Marxer Friedhof in Landstraße. In making this journey, I may not have found Marie-Thérèse in the way that I intended, but I did find her within my own mental projections onto the city, re-enacting, and literalising a process that Anthony Vidler has described as the spatial uncanny in his book *The Architectural Uncanny.*

The first place that I visited in Vienna was the House of Music at Seilerstätte 30, a museum devoted to an exploration of sound, and to the composers Beethoven, Schubert, and of course Mozart, the friend and contemporary of Marie- Thérèse von Paradis. One room in the museum tried to re-create the particularly uncanny experience of returning to the womb, generating sounds that a baby might hear. In 'The Uncanny', Freud suggests that the most *unheimlich*[33] place of all is the first, prenatal home of the womb, the entrance to the former home of all human beings, the place where each one of us lived, once upon a time, Kristeva's semiotic *chora* perhaps[34]. This Freudian theory informs my novel, because, in her later blindness, the character Marie seeks to return to such a womb-like state of being, a kind of fruitful darkness where she might nurture her own creativity. In this way, the character will also re-establish a state of oneness with her mother and with music.

Thus for Marie, loss of sight becomes a far more positive experience than the sublimated castration complex which Freud identifies in his discussion of Hoffmann's 'The Sandman'[35]. However, whilst Marie seems to find her creativity through her experience of physical confinement and darkness, a Freudian reading would emphasise the dangers of such regressive tendencies. Freud suggests that the desire to return to the womb functions as an inevitably unfulfilled desire for a retreat from life, which therefore renders it the potential crypt of living burial.

The room in the House of Music also recalls the uncanny myth of Amphion, who with his lyre caused the stones to join together to form the walls of Thebes. Schelling and Goethe likewise announce that 'architecture' is 'frozen' or 'petrified' music. The

House of Music also evokes Hoffmann's story 'Councillor Krespel,' in which an eccentric violinist lives in an equally eccentric house with haphazardly placed windows, not unlike those of Vienna's Hundertwasserhaus. Despite its haphazard nature, the foundations of Councillor Krespel's house were nevertheless erected on a perfect square. His house in fact suggests the relationship between architecture and music, whereby architecture is said, in its geometrical harmonies, to echo those of music. The house therefore replicates the musical personality of Councillor Krespel, his outer eccentricity and his inner soul.

Furthermore, Hoffmann's own creative process was not dissimilar to that of Councillor Krespel. In order to write, Hoffmann cultivated a special kind of composure, a *Bessenheit*, or mental state that controlled the release of images and translated stimuli from the outer world into the creative domain. By enacting this process, similar to my own in Vienna, the external world became a lever to set the inner world of the writer in motion.

It was nevertheless harder to enact such a process at Schönbrunn Palace, where the historical version of my protagonist had had music lessons with Salieri and audiences with the Empress. Despite these well-documented experiences, it was difficult to discover any trace of Marie at the Palace. In contrast, Mozart was everywhere. A four-year old Wolfgangeryl had even been painted into a picture of the wedding supper of Isabella of Parma and Emperor Joseph II, that is, *the Souper in the Reduite Halls* by Martin Van Meyer. However, Mozart was something of a retrospective ghost at the feast, since he would still have been living in Salzburg at the time of the wedding.

Mozart had also played for the Empress in the Mirrors Room, so-called because the Archdukes and Archduchesses had arranged the mirrors so that they created corridors reflecting unto infinity. Marie may also have played for the Empress in this room. Years later, the celebrated Doctor Mesmer, would treat her in a similar room at his clinic, believing that mirrors represented the opposite of blindness: that is, sight without touch.

However, it was apparent that at Schönbrunn, I could only find my character Marie through a process of associating her with other, more famous historical people. I was also striving and failing to make the Palace form my characters, developing an analytical yet passive receptivity reminiscent of Musil's Ulrich in *The Man Without Qualities*. Such attempts also evoke a related danger for the writer, that by projecting my associations onto the spaces around me, I ran the risk of only finding what I already knew. As Musil suggests in *The Man Without Qualities*:

> When one loves, everything is love, even when it is pain and loathing. The little twig on the tree and the pale windowpane in the evening light become an experience sunk in his own essential nature [...] a sensitive extension of his own body.[36]

In fact, like Musil's *The Man Without Qualities*, I was still searching for 'a magic formula, a lever that one might be able to get hold of, the real mind of the mind, the missing formula, perhaps very small, but that would close the magic circle.'[37]

This 'magic formula' also recalls the subject of my novel, Doctor Mesmer's attempt to restore the sight of a blind girl through a process similar to hypnosis. His attempts surely parallel those of a writer, who, in their work, creates images of space and place where before there were none. The next day, I therefore decided to go in search of Doctor Mesmer's mansion in the suburb of Landstraße. Earlier research suggested that Doctor Mesmer's address was 261 Landstraße, which my Viennese host interpreted as being 261 Hauptstrasse, that is, the High Street that runs through the suburb. A train, a bus, reading the numbers of the buildings, 180, 181, 182...and then the numbers stopped. No more Hauptstrasse. No Marie. No Mesmer. No magical, magnetic mansion.

The snow was falling as we turned down a side-road, when I suddenly saw a billboard which showed a young blond man holding a mask that was the exact replica of his own face. Freud, following Otto Rank, suggests that the doppelgänger is a harbinger of death. And so we entered the graveyard of Sankt Marxer Freidhof, where Marie- Thérèse von Paradis was buried.

In her novel, *Vienna Passion*, Lilian Faschinger describes a terrible dream her narrator experiences in which her dead mother demands to be dug up from the cemetery. The dead mother then picks up the narrator with her 'huge hands of worm-eaten flesh and porous bones, raised me to the level of the black holes that were once her eyes, and then opened her skeletal yellow jaws to swallow me.'[38] Freud notes that the uncovering of what has been buried not only offers a ready analogy to the procedures of psychoanalysis, but also exactly parallels the movement of the uncanny. Moreover, the dream which Faschinger describes occurs very early in the novel, in the first chapter, in fact. Perhaps then, the dream of digging up the dead mother also alludes to the writer's anxiety about digging up old memories to create a new narrative, and about the shape and form this narrative will take. Even Faschinger's adjectives of colour in this extract, 'black' and 'yellow' are also those of ink on paper…

I allude to Faschinger's novel as a means of trying to understand why my search for my protagonist led me to the graveyard. Like Dickens' Pip at the start of *Great Expectations*, staring at his parents' grave, perhaps I thought I could read Marie's character from the shape and style of the letters carved on her headstone.

And yet, once again, we could not find her.

Though we scanned the notice-board at the gate twice, she was neither listed with the composers, nor with the pianists. We were forced to search blindly, hoping for some affinity or instinct that would lead us to her grave. A cat waddled towards me through the snow, rubbed its head against my leg. I hoped that, like an animal in a fairy-tale, it would guide me there, but it didn't.

Then a woman emerged out of the snow, telling me, in German, that she was looking for the grave of Mozart. I told her that she needed the number from the notice-board, but she replied that the number was useless, since it didn't relate to anything. Then I explained that I was looking for the grave of Marie- Thérèse von Paradis, a friend and contemporary of Mozart's. She nodded, then walked away.

The thick snow gave a flat whiteness to everything, and the branches of the trees criss-crossed like an architrave.

A few moments later, the woman called me back. I walked towards her, hoping, hoping...but of course, it was Mozart's grave she'd found.

In his series of articles, *Hysteria and Enlightenment*, Roy Lisker describes how the real, historical Marie experiences instances of hypnagogic vision when she begins to recover her sight. This causes her to transpose one object onto her memories of another, like Proust perhaps, summoning up all of Combray from the steam of a teacup. Now, however, I longed for hypnagogic vision, so that I could somehow transpose Marie's grave onto Mozart's, to form her name out of the letters of his own. Because otherwise this moment in the graveyard seemed to encapsulate my entire experience of searching for Marie in Vienna. Wherever I looked for her, all I found was Mozart, always Mozart.

Marie herself experiences hypnagogic vision when she begins to recover her sight and tries to adapt herself to the seeing person's world. Likewise, when I visited the Freud Museum after the graveyard, I learned that Freud felt similarly unsettled when he was forced to move to London from Vienna, forced to communicate in a language that was not his own. However, Marie's and Freud's experiences surely parallel the more universal and uncanny experience of feeling rootless and unsettled wherever we are. The poet, Rainer Maria Rilke, a temporary citizen of

Vienna, once wrote in the first of the *Duino Elegies*, 'We are not really at home in our interpreted world.'[39] Perhaps this is why we try so hard to make ourselves feel at home, and secure. Is this also why writers attempt to write? To make ourselves feel at home whilst grappling with the fundamental sense of alienation and disorientation that we all experience? Rootless as we are, are we trying to ground ourselves in words, to create paper houses where before we had mansions of the mind?

However, it suddenly seemed that my own particular mansion of the mind, Doctor Mesmer's house in Landstraβe might actually exist. My Viennese host had discovered that there was a local history museum in Landstraβe whose curator, Professor Karl Hauer, knew the exact location of Doctor Mesmer's house, and possessed pictures of it.

I got lost on the way to the museum, and arrived snow-blind, breathless and late.

Professor Hauer nevertheless revealed the location of Mesmer's mansion, Rasumofskygasse 29, in Landstraβe, behind the post office, near the church. He also showed me an old engraving of it, its high turrets and towers just visible behind the trees, more like a palace than a mansion.

Of course, the mansion no longer exists. And when I asked Professor Hauer whether there would be a plaque on the site of Mesmer's house, he said no. He said that in Vienna, in Landstraβe, Mesmer had a very bad reputation. That there had been some kind of scandal with a young, blind pianist. That no-one was proud of him, that no-one wished to commemorate his existence. The founder of mesmerism does not have his own museum.

'The loss of the kingdom that was meant for me...'[40]

Surely that was how Mesmer must have felt, I thought, when he too was forced to leave Vienna after the scandal that ruined his reputation. Forced to leave his wife and mansion, with its beautiful rococo gardens, its folly, theatre and maze, his clinic, with its mirror-lined rooms, his fountain, that Marie used to call the 'Soup Tureen' where he healed assembled beggars and cripples. And, like Mesmer, I too felt I was an exile from these places, which had not been preserved and commemorated, which now, no longer existed. Nevertheless, we made our way towards Rasumofskygasse 29, now a shop doorway. And then, from across the square, the church bells began to chime. And I realised that Mesmer and Marie would have heard the same sound of bells, that perhaps they would even have incorporated it into his treatments and her music.

Then, in the museum of Vienna we found Joseph Huber's map of the city, which seemed to correspond to my own mental map. Entitled 'Bird's Eye View (Sceneography) of the City with its suburbs,' it was drawn in the same decade when Marie became a patient of Doctor Mesmer's, the 1770s. There was the church, and there, across the square, was his mansion, with its turrets and towers, its vast gardens.

And then, in the same museum, I saw an oil painting called the 'Interior View of a Viennese Freemason Lodge' from 1785. It depicted the bound eyes of 'the searcher.' Perhaps inevitably, this again recalled Marie, who, like the searcher, may know more and experience more in her own creative darkness than in the light which patriarchal notions of the norm attempt to impose on her.

Perhaps, during my time in Vienna, I too had become a searcher in a city of projected phantoms and thinking itself had become a kind of ghost seeing. On our final day in the city, we visited the Funeral Museum of Schlatthausgasse. Here we saw the Joseph Gemeindersarg, that is, a recyclable coffin introduced by the Emperor Joseph II from the year 1784. He ordered that bodies should be sewn into sacks, and then be made to fall out of the trap doors of the coffin into pits, where limestone would help them to decompose more quickly. This was the type of coffin used for Mozart's burial, giving rise to the myth of the pauper's funeral. The museum guide said that on Halloween, visitors were allowed to climb inside the coffin, a type of live burial which again evokes the Freudian uncanny. According to Vidler, the fascination exercised by burial alive, within the writings of Monk Lewis and Edgar Allan Poe, for example, may point to a specifically literary obsession with the buried utterance, the word, the tale, forever entombed without listener.

Freud also links the motif of burial alive with the desire to return to the womb, which takes us back to our starting place in the city, the womb-like room in the House of Music. Thus, in my time in Vienna, I had traced a circular trajectory following the Freudian uncanny from birth to death, discovering that the womb and the tomb were curiously linked, uncanny psychic spaces. As T S Eliot says in the 'Four Quartets': 'The end of all our exploring will be to arrive where we started, and know the place for the first time.'[41]

When you die in Vienna, they tie bells to your hands, so that if you are not really dead, you can ring the bell, and they will open up your coffin. Perhaps I too have attempted a similar process of resurrection, both within my searches through the city and in writing about them. Moreover, by sharing with you, the reader, this intimate fusion of mind and place, I have also re-enacted my own physical and mental journeys through the city.

Bibliography

Primary Sources:

Rubén, Dario, *The Selected Poems* translated by Lysander Kemp, University of Texas, Austin, 1988 http://www.dariana.com /R_Dario_poems.html#nocturne3 [accessed 9 February 2010].

Deutsch, Reinhard, ed. *House of Music Guide* (Horn: Druckeri Berger, 2000).

Dickens, Charles, *Great Expectations* (London: CRW Publishing 2003).

Eliot. T.S., 'Little Giddings', '4. Four Quartets' http://www. tristan.icom43.net/quartets/gidding.html [accessed 26 April

2006].

Faschinger, Lily, *Vienna Passion* in *Vienna, A Traveller's Literary Companion* (Berkely California:Whereabouts Press, 2008).

Freud, Sigmund, 'The Uncanny' in *The Uncanny* Translated by David McLintock, with an introduction by Hugh Haughton (London: Penguin Books, 2009)..

Hoffmann, E T A, *Tales of Hoffmann*, 'The Sandman' and 'Councillor Krespel' (Harmondsworth: Penguin Books, 1982).

Iby, Elfriede *Maria Theresa (1717-1780) Biography of a Monarch* (Innsbruck: Schloβ Schönbrunn, 2009).

Kristeva, Julia, *Revolution in Poetic Language* (New York: Columbia University Press, 1984).

Lachman, Gary, *Hypnogogia* www.forteantimes.com/features/articles/227/hypnagogia.html - [accessed 9 February 2010].

Lisker, Roy, *Hysteria and Enlightenment*, (a series of articles about Doctor Mesmer and Marie-Thérèse von Paradis) Ferment magazine www.fermentmagazine.org/HandE/MMT1.doc [accessed 9 February 2010]..

Musil, Robert, *The Man of No Qualities* (London: Secker and Warburg, 1979).

Rilke, Rainer Maria, The First Elegy of the Duino Elegies in *The Selected Poetry of Rainer Maria Rilke* edited and translated by Stephen Mitchell with an introduction by Robert Hass (Picador: London, 1987). p.151

Vidler, Anthony, *The Architectural Uncanny Essays in the Modern Unhomely*, (Baskerville: Massachusetts Institute of Technology, 1996).

Secondary Sources:

Bachelard, Gaston, *The Poetics of Space: an intimate look at how we experience Places*, (1958) Foreword by Etienne Gibson (Boston: The Beacon Press, 1969).

Bennett and Royle, Andrew and Nicholas,'The uncanny' in

Introduction to Literature, Criticism and Theory (Third edition Dorchester: Pearson Education Limited, 2004). Pp.34-42.

Brooks, Peter, *Reading for Plot Design and Intention in Narrative* (Harvard: Harvard University Press, 1992).

Brewster, Scott, 'Das Unheimliche [The Uncanny]' *The Literary Encyclopaedia*, (University of Salford: The Literary Dictionary Company), <http://www.litency.com/php.sworks.php?rec= true&VID=5735> [accessed 28 October 2005].

Daviau, Donald, ed. *Vienna, A Traveller's Literary Companion* (Berkely California: Whereabouts Press, 2008).

O' Doherty, Brian, *The Strange Case of Mademoiselle P* (London: Chatto and Windus, 1992).

Grosz, Elisabeth, 'Woman, *Chora*, Dwelling', in *Gender, Space, Architecture An interdisciplinary introduction* eds. Jane Rendell, Barbara Penner and Iain Borden (London: Routledge, 2000).pp. 210-22.

Kristeva, Julia, *Powers of Horror. An Essay on Abjection* trans. Leon S. Roudiez (New York: Columbia University Press, 1982).

McAfee, Noelle, *Julia Kristeva* (Routledge: New York and London, 2004)

Pick, Ronald, *Empress Maria Theresa* (New York: Harper and Row, 1966).

Royle, Nicholas, *The Uncanny* (Manchester: Manchester University Press, 2003.).

Welty, Eudora, 'Place In Fiction.' *On Writing.* (Toronto: Modern Library Edition, 2002).

With grateful thanks to Professor Karl Hauer, the curator of the Landstraße Municipal Museum, to Mag. Dr. Wittigo Keller, curator of the Bestattungsmuseum der Bestattung (Funeral Museum) in Vienna, to Nikolas Mayr our Viennese host, to Jana Kavkova, our hostess in Prague, to the inspirational Marco Cali, and to my supervisors at UEA, Professor Lavinia Greenlaw and Professor Lyndsey Stonebridge, as well as to Dr Rachel Potter.

The city exists in two states:
WALK DON'T WALK WALK DON'T WALK WALK WALK DON'T WALK WALK DON'T WALK WALK DON'T WALK WALK DON'T WALK WALK DON'T WALK WALK

Becky Cremin

When we evoke 'space,' we must immediately indicate what occupies that space and how it does so: the deployment of energy in relation to 'points' and within a time frame. When we evoke 'time,' we must immediately say what it is that moves or changes therein. Space considered in isolation is an empty abstraction; likewise energy and time.[42]

The city exists in two states:
WALK DON'T WALK WALK DON'T WALK WALK WALK DON'T WALK WALK DON'T WALK WALK DON'T WALK WALK DON'T WALK WALK

I want to examine these states. I want to explore the performance of the city by disrupting its rules. The city is a space of geometry, a space of paths, a space of walking, a space of don't walking. The city exists around us; I want to investigate my impact on this city. To explore the city in practice. To explore the city through performance. To explore the city and write from it. Michel de Certeau writes:

> Space is a practiced place. Thus the street geometrically defined by urban planning is transformed into a space produced by the practice of a particular place: a written text, i.e: a place constituted by a system of signs.[43]

For de Certeau, space is very much a constructed site, a site that is constructed by rules. A site which is formed of sign systems. A site I want to dismantle. De Certeau's series' of signs act as a text; the city is a textual site. The relationship then between the city and text is dependent on the operating of the geometry of the city. To dismantle the function of the city its textual order and geometry must be interfered with. De Certeau emphasises this geometry, this functionality of the city and we must be aware of it. The city is grid-like, the city fluctuates between, the city is online, the city is a text of signs and signifiers. The city is a written text waiting to be performed and exploded; waiting to be improvised.

De Certeau's definition of the city's structure must be realised, but the relationship between the city and the body is also one of importance. There is an exchange of energies between the body and the city; it is this relationship which is of great interest to me as a practicing artist. This relationship of exchange, hybridity and interdependence between the body and the city is investigated theoretically by Elizabeth Grosz. Grosz's definition of the city is one which works beyond de Certeau. She states:

> The city is a reflection, projection, or product of bodies[44]

Grosz's city is one of interdependence, one of co-dependence. We must be aware of this. We must consider this. We must understand the impact the body can have on site. We must understand the impact the site can have on body.

My practice is concerned with the exchange between the body and the city. How this exchange can be used as a way of investigating the city and its sign systems. How this exchange can expose the text of the city, how we can utilise it. How the city's language can be recycled and how the body can form new texts. Our urban textual landscape is built through these geometric sign systems; physical, bodily and metaphorical. The city's text is constructed of the bodies which inhabit it; the language these bodies produce and exchange. The city's text is constructed of the architecture which inhabits it; the code this architecture produces and exchanges. Both body and building leave a trace of their physicality, memory and signs systems on the city which surrounds us. The city then is a complex geometrical structure, which is working in multiple ways to communicate and construct its meaning.

The text of the city is constantly refreshing itself. The city's sign system is built of messages to DO, to BUY, to LOOK, to CROSS, to STOP, to CAUTION, to WALK, to DON'T WALK. The city's sign system is built of shop fronts, of cars, of people, of walk ways, of roads, of buses, of lights, of feet, of doors, of exits, of stairs, of ups, of concrete, of glass, of metal, it is built of symbols, signs which are all looking to influence and guide the body. The city's text is one which is constantly trying to communicate, to infiltrate the body. The city is a space in dialogue. The geometry of de Certeau has then become overloaded with signs, overloaded with systems and instructions. The twenty-first century city is an overloaded text and we must work harder than before to mediate and communicate it. The artist's body must find ways to negotiate this text and begin to find gaps in the city's geometry. Within the overloaded system there are opportunities to dismantle it; we must find spaces to move between the sign systems of the city and the body; to disrupt and re-order these signs. The question then becomes how to disrupt and re-order. How to perform the city?

There is a need for the body to interact, to force a reaction. I turn to the work of Carla Harryman, a poet who constructs poems plays essays prose through varied methods of rules and constraints. Her text *Performing Objects Stationed in the Sub World* investigates the status of language in performance. This text is constructed by Harryman site sampling[45] her home city of Detroit and uses language to explore a space. It is an act in 'the reordering of an already constructed text.'[46] Harryman is working with the city's geometry and by sampling from this she is providing a new version of the city and those who inhabit it. The relationship between site and language is very important in Harryman's work as she builds her own site through text:

> Pull the tree up you've got
> Sand
> No Shadow
> Push the sea back
> Sand
> No Shadow
> Up in the sky
> No sand
> No Shadow
> Water in the sky
> No Sand
> I am reminded of this...[47]

Harryman is working with found text, text she is extracting from the city's context and placing into her own work. She is dismantling and re-ordering the text of the city. This example taken from the opening of the play explores the shifting location; there is sand, there is no sand, there is water in the sky. Harryman is working with repetition to create an adjusted view and an adjusted geometry. This text is one made up from other bodies, signs, locations, movements; she listens, writes and performs. This method of production interests me. Yet it needs to be pushed further to enforce a dialogue between the city and the body.

BODY PERFORM THE CITY

I want to take what I need from the city and expel the rest; I want to recycle language. I want to work with the geometry of the city and sample from it and re-distribute these samplings. To dismantle a site through a physical interaction with it. I look to the work of Robert Smithson and his definitions of what a "site" and "non site" are. Site for Smithson is the area he collects from; this varies with each piece of work but usually involves a physical piece of the landscape being re-sited in the art space. His photographs in exhibition for example are often accompanied by an element from the landscape, (soil, a stone, and grass). Smithson's work focuses on the relationship between the physical sited entity and the art object. The non site is a remaking of the original site in a new place. Smithson's work raises interesting questions of space and its location and meaning. The removal of an object from one site to another forces the audience as well as the object to interact and perform in the new "non site". I wanted to explore how space becomes active due to interaction between:

space + performer
space + audience
space + time
space + art object
space + context
space + interactions

I return to the image of the city through de Certeau's eyes: the geometry. Our position and status in the city is a direct result of how our body reacts and interacts with the signs and signifiers in the city's mass of architecture. We are constantly refreshing our paths, we are constantly changing our route, we are constantly following directions. The human body in space occupies the position of spectator and spectacle and it is this relationship I wanted to examine. I wanted to become both spectator and spectacle. I wanted to invade my city; to act as a "bodily confrontation" [48] within it.

There I constructed my own method of interaction; I began to invade my own city. I invaded the space of others by placing an A1 piece of paper on the street; I then stood on Tottenham Court Road, London for two hours on Friday 7th March and recorded what went on around me. I became an intervention in the sign system, an obstruction, a full stop – change direction. I was an act in blocking the fluidity of the city. During this time I recorded the texts of the city – using a pen and paper – while being recorded myself on film. DON'T WALK. You WALK and then DON'T WALK. The geometry of the city's movement has been interfered with.

By engaging in physical acts of performance in the space of the city I am rethinking, re-organising and re-aligning expected values of the body, performance and the city's structures. My body is not aligning itself with the instructions of the city. It is not following its sign system, but creating my own. Grosz writes:

> If bodies are to be reconceived, not only must their matter and form be rethought, but so too must their environment and spatio-temporal location. [49]

Grosz is appealing for the "(re)finding and (re)situating" of the body within the city and the establishing of a 'parallelism between the body and the social order.'[50] This relationship between body and city would be one of dialogue and fluidity, and of material and corporeal dependence, with the two relating to and defining each other.

This relationship between text and body was utilised in the collection and construction of my text. The question then becomes: how to re-organise that text?

PERFORMANCE AS PRODUCTION

The production of the text, WALK DON'T WALK: a serial play, is an instance of body in interaction with the city. It contains instances of language which resist structure and linearity. WALK DON'T WALK: a serial play, is born out of a performance, of rupture and the text directly reflects this. The individual is lost in the text; instead it explores the body through instability and the possibility for repetition. It is this cultural construction which is ever present in my text: the sound of everyday conversation, locations, instructions, it's colloquialism. I hope the text sets up a discourse with its production methods as these methods not only construct it, but allow it to keep expanding in performance. WALK DON'T WALK: a serial play is a text which explores its production methods in live performance and looks to dismantle its own series of signs.

The dialogue between space and performer; space and object are continued in this piece's performance. I was concerned with the exchanges between practice and place and wanted this piece to not sit idly on a shelf. It was constructed through performance for performance. Nick Kaye discusses the 'environmental performances'[51] of Allen Kaprow, Claes Oldenburg and John Cage, these all examine the

Relationship between practice and place, and so work and site, fostering unpredictable, fluid exchanges between the frame of an artwork and its various contexts.[52]

It is these contexts which are key. WALK DON'T WALK: a serial play is an interdisciplinary exploration of not only space, but how text reacts to a space; how a site becomes a new site. It is not a piece of theatre, nor a poem; it is a play made to play with conventions and define its own site. I am interested in exploring the temporal implications of this piece on the performer, the audience and the text itself.

Let me explore the development of this piece in terms of performance further. WALK DON'T WALK: a serial play holds the ability to set up a dialogue between site and non site. The language confronts the public and exists in a liminal space between the real and the psychological. It is this BETWEEN which is important and it is this BETWEEN which is of interest in performance.

I became increasingly aware that this text was not precious to me. It was an improvised creation, it could be re-found in any city- in any space. This became important in performance. Again I return to the work of Carla Harryman, who states that the 'Theatrical space of the sub world becomes the public space of an inverted domestic space.'[53] I wanted to examine this "sub world" further, it is important to realise that this is a liminal space, a space of play:

Non linearity
Randomness
Collisions
Accidents

The "sub world" is a site where the object becomes the important being and status is destroyed. It is a site which looks to re-distribute text in a live experience and doing so re-evaluate the site and non site. The "sub world" is a 'site for other possibilities for narratives and conjunctions between subjectivities.'[54] It is a site which holds the possibility for deconstruction and reconstruction of the city's geometry. In reality when experimenting with this performance I wanted to create a performance which is influenced by the "sub world" and focuses on the object of text and performer. The city my text has been sampled from is one of hierarchies and in performance I was aware that I wanted to undermine these hierarchies and focus on a 'co-existence between performer and space.'[55]

In the most recent performance experiment of WALK DON'T WALK: a serial play, performed by four individuals, an actual performance space was taped to the floor and the performers were encouraged to interact with the text and each other. It was a durational experiment lasting forty minutes, lines echoed and re-used and obliterated. The text coming alive and reforming a new text:

The play is under construction.[56]

The performers did not follow a set script, instead using the text as a base for the performance. There is a shift in importance. The text precious on the page is destroyed in performance and redistributed into the world from which it came. The performance itself is a production of a new text.

This experiment, this practice based research is looking to dismantle the geometry of the city. To collect the city's fragmented sign systems and redistribute them. By interacting bodily with the city's textual landscape WALK DON'T WALK: a serial play is a new text which exposes the city's fragmentations. To write the city's text is to comment on the city. To dismantle the city's text is to dismantle the city.

To view **WALK DON'T WALK: a serial play** in text and performance please visit: http://serialplay.blogspot.com/

Bibliography

de Certeau, Michel. *The Practice of Everyday Life.* trans. Steven Rendall. London: University of California Press, 2002.

Grosz, Elizabeth. *Space, Time, and Perversion: Essays on the Politics of Bodies.* London: Routledge, 1995.

Kaye, Nick. *Site Specific Art: Performance, Place and Documentation.* London : Routledge, 2000.

Kennedy , David and Tuma, Keith. (eds.). *Additional Apparitions.* Sheffield: Cherry On The Top Press, 2002.

Lefebvre, Henri. *The Production of Space.* trans. Donald Nicholson-Smith. Oxford: Blackwell Publishing, 1991.

Can Writing Shape Place?

Sarah Butler

The stories that we tell matter because they indicate how we see the world, and whether we believe we have the power and capacity to shape it for the better. Stories are one of the main ways that we make sense of the world, and understand and interpret our lives and experiences. Stories and engaging people's imagination are potentially a powerful way to open up the futures of cities in democratic and creative ways.[57]

I am a writer, and also director of UrbanWords, a consultancy I set up in 2006 to explore how writing and writers might intersect with the process of regeneration. I am passionate about stories, and interested in how the stories we are able to tell about a particular place can have a tangible impact on that place's 'success'.

I take inspiration from Michel de Certeau's idea of space as 'practiced place': of the city as a place created by the complex actions and interactions of its inhabitants.[58] My understanding of place is that it is inextricably linked with the people who live in and pass through it. I believe that as humans we understand place, our relationship to it, and to other people, through story: the stories we tell, hear, invent and hold about places. I would argue that our relationship to the places we know is imbued with, and constructed through, narrative.

I run participatory, community-based projects, which look to explore, unpick and articulate communities' relationships to their environment. I partner with local authorities, architects and planners to find ways to bridge the 'communication gap' between urban regeneration professionals and the communities they are working with. I have a particular interest in co-authorship, and how writers might work with communities, planners, architects and developers to create new co-authored stories for urban spaces.

I am not interested in using good writing and storytelling as a marketing tool. I am interested in how we might harness this idea of story, as a way of understanding place, as a way of communicating that understanding, and as a way to help make places better. I am interested in how stories can be unlocked and created by the people who live in and use places, with and alongside, the people who make and change these places. I am interested in how this work can enable people to communicate with architects, planners, and developers, so that they start to feel that they have agency over and responsibility for the places they use.

This essay will address three main ideas. Firstly that writing, and participatory writing projects, can enable people to explore and understand their relationship to space more fully and complexly. Secondly that writing, and in particular creative writing and story-telling, is an ideal medium in which to articulate and communicate that understanding to those involved in changing and developing our urban spaces. And thirdly, that stories can act as a powerful tools of change and transformation: if we tell a new story we open up a new space, we create the possibility for change to happen.

Exploring, understanding and owning place

Early on in my explorations into the world of urban regeneration, I had a conversation with a planning consultant about how his company put together 'character profiles' of a place. It became apparent that their methods included archive research and walking around the area, but did not include talking to anyone. I was horrified that decisions were being made about the nature of a place with no reference to the experience of living or working there. It also struck me that there was potentially a real role here for arts projects and artists, who could spend the time, and have the skills, to really get to the bottom of a place, to observe it and unpick it, through conversation and creative work with communities. I recognised too, the potential for this work to be much more complex and in depth than traditional consultation methods.

This work has a significant additional dimension when it is approached in a participatory way. By engaging local people in a creative exploration of their places, their relationship with that place will inevitably change. A couple of years ago I spoke to a participant in a project being run by the poet, Linda France.[59] Linda had been leading creative writing workshops in Durham Cathedral, and the woman I spoke to told me how spending time looking at and creatively responding to the cathedral changed her relationship with it: 'I feel like I own it now,' she said.[60]

In the autumn of 2008 I was writer-in-residence on the Greenwich Peninsula in East London, with the poet Aoife Mannix.[61] We ran open and targeted writing workshops, interviewed local residents and employees and wrote our own new work in response to the place. The project had two key outcomes: a sound piece combining our own work with the voices and stories of local people,[62] and a temporary hoarding piece by the artist Faisal Abdu'Allah, which incorporated a poem written by myself and year 3 students from the local primary school. This poem was particularly well received by the developers of the site, who printed it in their staff newsletter.[63]

A Walk on the Greenwich Peninsula, by Lichtenstein Class 3 at Millennium Primary School (short version on hoardings light-box)

We saw blurry reflections of colourful houses,
Smelt dark green water and cool fresh air,
Heard the sound of a plane, and a sound like a bell,

Felt the breeze, the soft leaves, the smooth silver poles,
We felt warm, laughing, brilliant, happy.

Blog entry, Sarah Butler, 29th October 2008

We could go for a walk together some day, you and me. I'll
show you the secret places, if you ask right. The empty space
behind the hoardings in the square, where grass creeps up
between stones, and buddleia blooms pink amongst the grey.
The field behind Sainsbury's where the skylarks sing. We'll
reach down and touch the grass, crunch leaves between our
fingers to find out what green smells like. There are treasures
on the beach if you take the time to look. If you're not the kind
of person who likes talking, we can just sit and listen. The
barges sound like thunder. The boats sound like bells. There
are birds that've flown half way across the world to be here.

Consultation is one of those deeply charged words I tend to
mumble and feel uncomfortable about, but I think there is a
really interesting and important role for the arts and creativity
within this field. In the summer of 2009, I was lead artist on a
project called *My Place*, working with a number of artists to
engage young people in a conversation about a new performing
arts space being created in North London. The aims of the project
were two-fold – to gather ideas and aspirations for the space
from young people and communicate those to the architects and
the council, and to build the young people's relationship with the
space in the years leading up to its opening. The building is due
to open in 2011, and the young ambassadors we worked with are
still closely involved in its development.

I recently commissioned the writer Chris Meade to write a
thought piece about the creative consultation work he does with
the artists and designers *Snug and Outdoor*. Both he and Hattie
Coppard, director of *Snug and Outdoor*, talk about the fact that if
you ask children what they want in a playground they'll say

swings and a slide, and can they be green, or red, or blue. In other words they will describe playgrounds they have already seen. If you take them through a creative process that asks them what is play? What makes them feel safe, excited and so on, then you get very different answers that enable you to create very different playgrounds. The challenge, and I think it is one that artists can particularly rise to, is how to get people to imagine something they have never imagined before.[64]

Articulating and Describing Place

Every sector has a language and jargon that comes along with it, and Regeneration is no exception. However, I think that this is an area where it is really important that that language – that path to communication – is opened up, because the decisions that are being made impact directly on people's environments and lives.

It seems to me that writers are particularly well placed to play a role here: in finding ways to articulate and describe places. Writers are able, are indeed trained, to capture complex information and ideas and express them in a way that people can connect with.

I did a project with *muf Architecture/Art* in Barking a couple of years ago. *muf* were commissioned by Design for London to create an exhibition to inform local residents about the huge number of building projects taking place in their town centre. The exhibition, *Barking, a Model Town Centre*, was a series of architects' models, and *muf* wanted to find a way to make those models accessible and understandable to local people. I worked with the poet, Aoife Mannix, to run workshops with local people, looking at the imagined occupations of these new buildings. The texts they created (example below) were used next to the architects' models, instead of traditional construction information.

I'd have a café with huge sofas and bottomless coffee pots, sell homemade carrot cake and chocolate chip cookies. There'd be free newspapers and old fashioned ceiling fans, books too. The staff would chat to you about politics and love, tell you that drinking coffee and dreaming are far more important than making money or worrying about what other people think. That life is short but afternoons are long, and good company is priceless.[65]

It was a small scale project, but I loved the idea that we could use story and creative expression to enable people to look at an architect's model and imagine themselves in that space. Liza Fior from *muf*, commented about this and other projects:

Visions, masterplans and finally buildings begin with an executive summary and end with an Operations and maintenance manual. Sarah Butler explores the pre life, the afterlife and repercussions of change through language - language, far, far, away from the jargon of regeneration and so much more accurate.[66]

Effecting Change

The quote at the beginning of this paper is one which I find particularly inspiring. It's from the book, *The Dreaming City: Glasgow 2020 and the Power of Mass Imagination*, which came out of an 18 month project run by the think tank Demos. *Glasgow 2020* took the idea of story as a powerful tool of change and transformation and applied it on a city-wide scale to Glasgow. From creative writing workshops, to large scale participatory events, thousands of potential stories for Glasgow were collected and then analysed and interpreted into concrete proposals for the future of the city.

I've been thinking a lot recently about whether writing and stories can change a place. I think there are two aspects to consider, the first of which is to do with perception and emotion, and the second with physicality.

Stories can be immensely powerful, emotionally, and can leave us with strong responses to places we've never even visited. I remember reading *Brighton Rock* as a teenager and being convinced that Brighton was a dark and dangerous place. It's only in the last couple of years that I've discovered it as a delightful, light-filled city. Look, too, at what *Clockwork Orange* did for Thamesmead. These are negative examples, but I think we can turn them on their heads and explore how through creative engagement and expression, we can work to shift people's relationship with a place, which in turn can change how that place operates and is perceived.

Michael de Certeau talks about stories as spatial practices which have the transformative power of metaphor.[67] I believe that if we tell a new story we open up a new space, and we create the possibility for change to happen. In the summer of 2009, I was commissioned by the architecture practice, *PublicWorks*, to write a new fiction for a stretch of the Leeds-Liverpool Canal, which formed the focus of Liverpool Biennial's 5 day conference, Urbanism 09. The story was commissioned to sit alongside a temporary structure, designed by *PublicWorks*, called the Canal Club – a floating space for conversation and debate. My aim was to explore the potential of a place which is frequently dismissed as a 'wasteland'. The story is called 'Fishing For Stars' (inspired by the star-shaped lanterns attached to the 'Club'). It follows three characters, Caib, Rhaw and Bywell (their names are drawn from a mural of ancient tools painted on one of the canal's walls) who all discover their own routes into a magical parallel universe, where their wishes for the canal come true. Vinyl-cut extracts from the story were installed onto the Canal Club itself, copies were hung by the seating areas, and visitors were given copies to take away.[68]

So, perhaps writing can change perceptions of a place, but can it change place physically? There is an interesting example where the ideas behind storytelling have been transposed into the physical design of a space. The poet and writer, Chris Meade suggested to *Snug and Outdoor* that they might use the key elements of narrative within their playground designs. So a play space would have a pathway, a threshold, a sanctuary, a destination, and an arena to perform in. His idea was that these elements would provide suggestive spaces that inspire creative play. The built environment would hold the structures to inspire the narratives which help us relate to and understand place and our position within it. Hattie Coppard, Director of *Snug and Outdoor*, says that this thinking has radically changed how they approach playground design. The concept of narrative and its different elements is now key to their thinking when they design new spaces.

What's in it for the writer?

I am passionate about the role writers can play in making places better to live, work and play in. However, I think it is essential that art and regeneration projects achieve a balance between the art and the regeneration. Projects need to avoid becoming solely about the regeneration agenda, with art being 'used' as a tool, rather than respected and celebrated for what it is: art. There has to be a reason for the writer to be involved, it has to do something for their own practice and development.

On a personal level, I work in this area for a variety of reasons. I am fascinated by the relationship between place and people: the impact it has on our emotions, our aspirations, and our relationships. I also have a fascination with how place is made, and I think lots of artists working in the field share a fascination with the idea of construction. Artists make things, builders make things; the Scottish word for poet is Makar. There is a real connection between the process of writing and the process of construction.

Regeneration is about change, and with change comes conflict and drama, which is the stuff of literature. I often teach creative writing, and am constantly talking about finding the conflict, upping the stakes, thinking about what change happens within story, so I see thematic links between this idea of story and Regeneration. It works on a more formal level too: metaphor is about change, and it is the writer's most powerful tool: this ability to transform one thing into another and in doing so find meaning.

I am hugely interested in and nosy about people: their motivations, their relationships, what they say and what they don't say. I think this links interestingly with the concept of consultation. Consultation is about discovering what people think about a place and how they want to improve it. If a writer has been trained to listen to what isn't being said, to discover the motivations behind people's words and actions, then surely there is a way for them to contribute to meaningful consultation?

As a writer, I have a desire to communicate, and an obsession with language, and Regeneration offers a particularly rich field within which to operate. I am interested in, and passionate about the social role of art, and want to be an artist who plays a positive role in society.

To conclude, I see a real potential for writers to meaningfully engage with Regeneration and urban change through creative engagement and participatory projects; projects which explore people's relationship to place, and through that process build, change, and challenge that relationship. Writers can find ways to describe and articulate place and people's relationship to it in a way that can be responded to by designers, architects, and urban planners. And finally I believe that story is a powerful agent of change, and that writers can find ways to tell new stories which can open up the possibility of positive change for places and communities.[69]

Bibliography

Tims, Charlie; Hassan, Gerry; Mean, Melissa. *The Dreaming City*. Demos, 2007

de Certeau, Michel. (trans. Steven Randall) *The Practice of Everyday Life*, University of California Press, 1988

www.sarahbutler.org.uk

www.urbanwords.org.uk

Interstitial Practices and 2 *Ennerdale Drive:* *unauthorised biography*

Rosa Ainley

The darkness of the entrance, the arched portico and glass-paned door, the privet-edged path all seems so familiar. They beckon me in. I can pretend that I'm recognising this house, over the many others like it whose front paths I have walked up in other north London suburbs. Like memorists of antiquity I use the hedge and porch as prompts for where I am in the story, to substitute place as memory. So I'm looking for remembrance still. The hall light is off and the curtains are drawn, even though it's hardly dark yet. I knock with the letterplate handle. Long pause.

I say beckon me in, but it doesn't. The house is set up for the opposite effect. It's semi-detached, for a start. I'm just ignoring the warning signs. Not everybody needs to have a dog. It's not like I really remember any of this but something's being mapped out. There's no getting away with dawdling up that garden path. It's straight up and down, single file and don't touch the hedge. Intruders are repelled by layout alone. That sneaky glazed portico deliberately gives the wrong impression: there's no transparency like the false promise of see-through glass, no transparency at all. It's obscurity, and one-way at that. No need for fortifications, with a frontage like this; the whole place is a characterisation of them. Inside and out, it's all façade. Nobody's feeling at home here. Somewhere a big cork stopper interrupts the tidal flow of lived existence, chamber upon chamber of cellar space, an archive of life unlived.

I'm thinking that I shouldn't have come, that I should have come ten years ago, that I should have come at any time during the last 20 years, but not now. The pause gets longer and I bang the handle again sharply. I try to look through the spy mirror even though I know it's only there to look back at me, not the other way about.

Without warning of footsteps or lights coming on, the door is opened a little, so I'm surprised and say nothing. There's silence and a wave of interior pours out. She peers at me, as though groggy. She doesn't know who I am. Advantage me, but it doesn't feel like one. All I want is – well, what? To come inside and what then? As if I want to be ushered into the front parlour as the prodigal great-niece and send out for a Fuller's walnut cake.

Any second she'll go 'Yes?' or 'Not today, thank you.' I can't see inside but I can tell she's very, and strangely, well dressed. I half expect her to be wearing hat and gloves. So I haven't interrupted the spring-cleaning. Then again, she could be doing just that, the suburban lady making light of her work. A knock at this door is never going to be anything other than an interruption. There is no mat on my side of the front door and it would not say welcome. Instead a metal grille sits in front of the step to stop cattle or anything else crossing the threshold. She's opened the door a crack more, enough to let me sidle in, no grand gestures here. It's a privilege nonetheless. I give her my card so she can see the name in print but she's still not having it and peers at it as if to detect forgery. I'm not who I say I am. I almost say 'Don't you know who I am?' but I can tell she's not going to fall for that. And who am I to her, after all? There's no connection, whichever way you look at it: wrong side of the family, wrong generation, wrong decade, wrong gender too I expect. The lot.

A house of small, disconnected containments, we stand just inside the hall, breathless in the airlock, keeping me separate from her privacy in this antechamber, closer than either of us would like to be. She bars my way to penetration further into the house without doing a thing. The hall will have to tell me all I need to know, as it does for most of the visitors. She's already told me that he's out. Now she says, 'We're having our evening meal,' but I can't smell anything except dank furnishings and she's not going to tell me who's joining her for dinner. Her imaginary friend Johnny Walker, I'd say. I'm lucky she's not going to invite me to join them.

In the corner, by the very closed door of the front sitting room, is a small telephone table, its appliance resting on a bleak square of threadwork that must have been made under better lighting than this. The kitchen door at the end of the corridor is panelled in glass and shielded from any inquiries by its pattern. The life of the house needs protection from more than my gaze. Everything is so protected it's entirely exposed: the hall runner by a plastic overlay, covered in turn by a doorway mat; secrets screened by the dim yellow light.

From the street side the front door is wreathed in light and glass. Some effort has gone into mitigating this effect indoors. The runner continues up the staircase, but no plastic sheathing is needed there apparently. It's like a b&b where access to bedrooms is a policing matter. I turn around the long way as I leave, to get a glimpse of what I hadn't been able to see before. This is as far as your road goes. The same wallpaper is hung up the stairway, its floral pattern as pretty as the neighbourhood they, the suburban dwellers, imagined they would live in, now all faded, colours and warmth long gone. I can't see any more than this, there's no delaying. Whatever I want, I'm not welcome. I'm looking, looking in, that's insult enough to merit closed doors. With a goodbye so polite it blisters, I'm out again to be guided down the privet strait to take me safely off the premises. I breathe. Inside, there's no reason to stop holding on.

2 Ennerdale Drive: unauthorised biography, Chapter 1, Telling Tales[70]

2 Ennerdale Drive: unauthorised biography is a memoir of an existing suburban family house in northwest London built in the 1920s. The book sets up and explores architectural narrative and its place in the construction of social, political and personal histories. It analyses the everyday lived experience of housing design through the prism of a constructed family narrative, disturbing the boundaries of the imaginary and the real. The family tale is rooted in the physicality of the building: the tale, highly contestable, while the building is apparently factual. The tale involves members of my own family – the awkwardness of my position in playing the roles of author and character drives one strand of narrative in the book.

The opening extract describes the experience of trying to gain access to the house and therefore family, and reaching no further than the hall. With an interest in liminal spaces, I note that descriptions of house often skip past the hall and move straight from front door to living room. The amount of space involved may be inconsiderable; the significance of the hall space in general and in particular at no.2 Ennerdale Drive is that it is a decompression chamber between exterior and interior, between public and private lives. To some extent the hall operates as a metonym for the suburb as a whole, which is similarly laden with imperatives about separation, keeping yourself to yourself, and maintaining very rigidly imagined borders between an us and a them. The hall could, of course, also be a site of welcome and acceptance.

In *2 Ennerdale Drive: unauthorised biography* I am both

excavating and originating my own family history: it is less genealogy than fabrication, less revisionist than visionist. Observations on the architectural and social history of suburban development of the period are intercut with the imagined and the fictional. In the process, I am creating another version of memoir, neither family history nor novel, although it employs some of the strategies and tropes of both. In this book in particular I have employed a variation on Gaston Bachelard's 'topoanalysis', 'the systematic psychological study of the sites of our intimate lives'.[71] I explore the overlooked, the taken-for-granted, digging down to recover the uniqueness of the everyday, re-presenting it from an altered angle, a shifted perspective. It has been described as a poetics of the ordinary.[72]

This essay explains some aspects of the development of interstitial practices and shows how they operate in the book. The intention is to reflect upon and question ideas that underlie my work while also being reflexive, to consider the role I play as practitioner, using extracts from the book to frame critical exploration of its ideas and process and my practice generally. In offering commentary on how a writer might construct spatial narratives, it gives insight into the approach of this writer in interdisciplinary practices that allow the crossing of borders and, to paraphrase Rosi Braidotti, the theorising of fictions and the fictionalising of theory.[73]

Architecture tells stories, it exists on paper. Writing creates spaces, which tell stories too of buildings and architecture and those who use it, see it and make it. Notions of performance and narrative, absence and presence, aspiration and separation, intimacy and exposure, solidity and fragility, community and individuality attach to both building and stories. In my work I'm writing the building and constructing the story, and examining the divide between them, the interstice. Clearly writing is an act of construction; in this case there is a physical structure and an architecture of stories too. In recent years I have written for print and digital production about spaces including an airport, a community hall, waiting rooms, an Airstream trailer, bridges, a visitor centre, a PortaKabin, a house, a promenade and aural spaces. Whether these subject-spaces are physical or imaginary, textual or architectural, the work stands under the banner of what Jane Rendell calls site-writing, which she defines as involving poetic practice and theoretical analysis.[74] I share Rendell's interest in the porosity of boundaries between subjects and disciplines, calling into question methodologies and terminologies.

I am engaged then in creating or revealing what I call interstitial spaces, by which I mean those spaces that cross or allow the crossing of borders, which are in-between categories. The transitional and the speculative form the subject; they are also methodology in that the work proceeds through an exploration of the architectonics of writing: the structure, processes and materials employed become part of the subject. My practice might be described as existing in the interstices between fields such as architecture and literature, critical and creative writing (also known as art writing), irrigating highly territorialised borders between proximate subjects. More than the spaces I'm working with and the practices I use to describe them, interstitial also works as a description for where I situate myself as a writer/artist. I'm writing spaces and writing about spaces, writing the visual and auditory and documenting the visual and auditory. I write a space for myself to occupy.

The work of the architect and the writer proceeds in very different ways but both writing and architecture start by imagining the unimaginable, giving it form, pinning it down to some extent, at least long enough to draw it or write it. Architecture is remade through use, a story is remade with every telling. Like the architect, the author may play many different roles. In 2 *Ennerdale Drive* the list of these has included: detective, archaeologist, reporter, archivist, researcher, documentarist, spieler, bit-part player, shape-shifter, director. The role of the architect has legal duties to fulfil that the writer does not but both need to construct something that will stand up, whatever its material.

When I embarked on the book I had been engaged in developing a digital writing practice, working on multimedia projects in the previous few years, adding use of sound to the mix of text and image. I planned the book to be a work entirely of words and in print. As the book took shape, it enabled me to bring together my written and visual practices – almost as though the structure of the book demanded it, as a fictional character might take on a mind of its own. To use Esther Leslie's description of Walter Benjamin's work here, using text and image, and text *about* image, allows me to 'tap transformative potentials embedded in actuality [to] synthesise connections and disruptions.'[75] The use of visual materials gives the book a skeleton, and also introduces the idea of transparency and obscurity in representation, how images simultaneously tell truths and fictions.

2 *Ennerdale Drive* questions the veracity accorded to 'documents' produced across institutional, public and private family contexts. The 'picture texts' collected from various archives are a series of publicity stills and other advertising materials and a single family photograph; these relate to the house, the family and its business: theatre. Textual analyses of these images frame each chapter, generating stories and responses to the factual and the remembered, suggesting strongly the entanglement of domestic and professional lives. Deconstructing these images highlights the insubstantiality of family memories. Some of these are attached to publicity relating to the public life of the professional stage; the power of advertising is also evident in the items publicising the benefits of the suburbs, and this public/private dualism runs throughout the book.

I am cultivating a distinct lack of certainty in the book, along with ambivalence about my own position in the narrative I am interrogating and refashioning. Even the family credentials referred to in the opening excerpt are open to question. It is a work about ambivalence, rather than a pursuit of the definitive tale – this is a family history that is rewritten by each telling. Architectural space – the stone or brick – is not static. Like a family story it is changed by use, personal or social investment and memory. The most ephemeral, the story on paper or held in the imagination, can become the most enduring. As the book unpicks the perceived certainties of suburban life represented in the house, it shadows the equivocations of the family tale.

The house is a backdrop; it is as insubstantial as a hanging paper flat in an auditorium, yet it is the hard nucleus of the book. None of the rest could exist without it. The house is itself a theatre, a domestic stage and a trigger for remembering and for inventing situations and events. It is above all a useful tool to map the outskirts of some family geography as well as the architectural and social history of its context, while also being the built object I need as a writer to play out this disruption of memoir. No.2 Ennerdale Drive is a construction twice over on which to hang my own; to bring in the wider world, rope in and peg down ideas and my version of stories. Bachelard calls the house 'the theatre of the past', and this is an irresistible description to me given that the family profession at no.2 is theatre, and so both public and private lives are played out onstage.[76] For the domestic stage though, in that house and all the others built in suburbs across the country, scripts were allotted by developers, policy makers and architects, to dictate and legitimise certain lifestyles and behaviours.

Suburban architecture insists on a social commentary, both as an interwar phenomenon and precisely because it is a style reviled within architectural criticism yet chosen by the majority of households in the UK. Divisive and inclusive then, suburban development of the 1920s invokes issues of social mobility, architecture and building, gender roles and class. Complex narratives of aspiration, separation and change are played out. 2 *Ennerdale Drive: unauthorised biography* is drawing attention to what is unspeakable and unspoken, aiming to unfold the space around it, rather than necessarily trying to vocalise it. Sales materials for early 20th century suburban houses (examples are used as image texts in the book) often included assurances about the 'hygienic' properties of the area and its 'good drainage'. These can be read as coded allusions to restrictions against undesirable working-class people moving in. At the same time, part of the drive to build and inhabit the suburbs was recognition of the need for fresh air and green space to improve the poor health levels revealed in First World War recruitment halls. If the suburbs operate as a performative space of domesticity and architecture, clearly these are highly gender-specific. The book expatiates on the ways in which women living in the suburbs were expected to conform to problematic and often contradictory roles. The domestic angel had to be seen to enjoy staying at home and using new labour-saving devices, the employee was making an essential – if counter to the mythology – contribution to funding the perceived step up in family status to home ownership.

The suburbs are then not as homogenous, on various levels, as they are usually portrayed, any more than social housing is. Lynsey Hanley's narrative account offers a recent example of work that debunks this, here in relation to post-Second World War housing estates.[77] Although I imagine and expose the stories that architecture tells us in my work (the fractured narratives that are woven into architecture, and those that are written on the body), I avoid attempting to read off the building. I'm intending instead to disrupt any perception of an analogous relationship between society and its built form, rather laying bare fictions and floorboards, exposing discontinuities and creating others.

2 *Ennerdale Drive: unauthorised biography* exposes as over-simplified and misleading the convictions of the suburban, as it

exposes the impossibility of the rounded, shared family tale. The suburb can be viewed as a form in a state of permanent insecurity marked indelibly on to it, defining it as it defines itself always against what it is not: the urban. In contrast to this the interstitial practice revels in its status. The hall at no.2 might be the threshold, a transition towards the edge of a new practice. Instead of always stepping across the threshold from one to other, from here to there, from now to then, I am deliberately occupying that space between. The suburb is, in a sense, neither one thing nor the other. Interstitial practice and *2 Ennerdale Drive: unauthorised biography* as an example of it, is positioned as both one thing and the other.

2 Ennerdale Drive is an ordinary, mid-size semi, built by John Laing and Co in 1926 and inhabited by members of the same family until 2005. A blink of an eye, you might say, or a lifetime span. In a family for whom discontinuity is the pattern, where a life spent in the same country or even continent has been unusual, where relocating seemed to be the norm, the existence of 2 Ennerdale Drive could cast a net of reassurance across the narrative.

In a full-frontal view, that overlooking window panel of next door's bow is peeking into the frame: oh no you don't, I'm here too you know, don't think you can forget me. This intrusion, this shameless waving at the camera, also indicates how the design of the house works. The ambiguities inherent in the semi-detached suburban are immediately apparent. There's no place for the dividing line between the semis to sit happily. The house is desperate to be singular, individual, as they all are, yet it's the same as the one next door, only transposed. It's attached, semi, but making an effort to pretend to be detached by placing its front door as far away from the other house as the building can stand. A side section of its bow window, on both ground and first floors, faces the same window next door. It's always there.

There is no way to see this building or even to take a photograph of this house, half or whole, entire or split, one way or the other. So the impression and the house itself, , can never be quite satisfactory. It's impossible to see the whole house without seeing the other, the let's-pretend-it's-not-there, the same but completely alien, house. The house is never quite finished as a structure, it can only ever be a half. Never finished as a home either, anyone would think.

The family bought the house new and it passed through three generations of unmarried ownership, from great-aunt to mother to son. Colindale didn't exactly 'spring up' like a seasonal eruption of early suburb in north London. It was squeezed into existence through a coincidence of temporal and spatial circumstances and responses – war, pollution, snobbery, legislation, class hatred, desire, business, innovation and tradition, reaction and technology.

2 Ennerdale Drive might be imagined as a sanctuary against: the town, the neighbours, the missing family, the world. Its windows, far from the picture window of the viewing mechanism and of the film screen, emulate the small divided panes of an earlier age before the manufacture of larger sheets of glass became possible. The very tectonics of the house constitute an event: the event of suburban construction. The window breaks up the view into segments – shards of the outside world miniaturised into unthreatening sections. Postcard-size, safe missives from elsewhere. This is no accident: the design of the house gives the framework for a lifestyle, both the public march morning and evening to the train station and the private – the new forms of domestic role-playing. This is building as projection.

This suburban domesticity is a performance whose audience may not exist for it beyond its own players. The intention was never to create an experimental stage to try out new forms of production; it was designed around an ideal of containment and a coercion of the arts of town planning and architecture.

A suburban house is like a playhouse. A facsimile of house, its inhabitants are playing a pre-scripted role on a set, while watching themselves do it, smiling, with self-approval or is that uncertainty?

2 Ennerdale Drive: unauthorised biography, Chapter 2, Private Lives

Bibliography

Bachelard, Gaston, *The Poetics of Space*, Boston, Mass.: Beacon Press, 1994

Braidotti, Rosi, *Nomadic Subjects: Embodiment and Difference in Contemporary Feminist Theory*, New York: Columbia University Press, 1994

Carter, Angela, *Wise Children*. London, Chatto & Windus, 1991

Certeau, Michel de, *The Practice of Everyday Life*. Berkeley, University of California Press, (1988).

Colomina, Beatriz, *Privacy and Publicity*. Cambridge, Mass. And London. MIT Press, 1996

Hanley, Lynsey, *Estates: An Intimate History*, London: Granta Books, 2007

Kuhn, Annette, *Family Secrets*. London, New York, Verso, 1995

Leslie, Esther, 'Telescoping the Microscopic Object: Benjamin the Collector' in *The Optic of Walter Benjamin*, edited by Alex Coles, London: Black Dog, 1998

Nobus, Dani, Who am I? *The Ego and the Self in Psychoanalysis*. B. Seu. London Rebus Press, 2000

Rendell, Jane, *Art and Architecture: A Place Between*, London and New York: IB Tauris, 2006

Russell, C. 'Autoethnography: Journeys of the Self', excerpt from *Experimental Ethnography*, Duke University Press. Available at: www.haussite.net

Ryle, Martin, John McGahern: 'Memory, Autobiography, Fiction' in *Reading Life Writing New Formations*. London. Lawrence and Wishart, 2009

Steedman, Carolyn, *Dust*. Manchester, Manchester University Press, 2001

Steedman, Carolyn, 'On Not Writing Biography' in *Reading Life Writing New Formations*. London. Lawrence and Wishart, 2009

Todorov, T, *The Poetics of Prose*. Blackwell. Oxford, 1977

Turkington, R. and Ravetz, A., *The Place of Home: English Domestic Environments 1914–2000*. London. Chapman + Hall, 1995

The Brutalist School: A Lefebvrian Poem

Gavin Goodwin

In this essay I would like to discuss the possibility of a
relationship between architecture and poetry, particularly in
instances where there is a gap between the ideals of the architect
and the lived experience of the user; or in the terminology of the
Marxist philosopher, Henri Lefebvre, the gap between *representations of space* and *spaces of representation*.[78] I have written a poem
exploring these issues with reference to one building in
particular, Newport High School,[79] in South Wales, a prize-
winning Brutalist structure that was demolished in 2010. This
essay will discuss some of the thinking behind Brutalism and
why it is sometimes held in contempt within the working-class
communities in which its buildings are often situated. I will go
on to discuss how poetry might engage with this problem, and
give examples of my own attempts to do so.

New Brutalism, a late development and reaction against some
earlier forms of Modernist architecture, became fashionable in
Britain during the 1950s and became for a time the state architecture of choice. It was/is characterised by 'exposed rough
concrete finishes and chunky, blocky forms'. It was influenced by
the post-war works of Le Corbusier, especially his *Unité
d'Habitation*, in Marseilles (1948–54), a block of flats 'in which
béton brut was treated particularly uncompromisingly, with the
formwork patterns not only visible, but deliberately empha-
sized'.[80] The Brutalists had, in the words of Alison and Peter
Smithson, a 'respect for materials – a realisation of the affinity
which can be established between buildings and man',[81] which is
why surfaces were often untreated. Their style was also influenced by Mediterranean peasant buildings. The Brutalists saw in
these buildings 'an anonymous architecture of simple rugged

geometrical forms [...] unaffectedly and immemorially at home in its landscape setting.'[82] Another important characteristic of Brutalism, again following Le Corbusier, was an emphasis on functionalism. That is, for the Brutalists, form followed function; Brutalism, in the Smithsons' view, was an ethic rather than an aesthetic.

Although Brutalist buildings vary considerably, they are all likely to be informed to some degree by the concerns mentioned above. Newport High School, a Brutalist building by Eldred Evans and David Shalev,[83] conforms broadly to these criteria. Built between 1968 and 1971 at the tail-end of Brutalism's reign, it is a clear example of the style – raw concrete blockwork, with an emphasis on circulatory patterns that operate via systems of steps and networks of corridors. Although the building never achieved the fame of the Smithsons' Hunstanton Brutalist school, when Newport High School was threatened with demolition there was a campaign, led by The Twentieth Century Society, to save it (Richard Rogers, among others, was a vocal opponent of its destruction). The building, however, was refused listing, due in part to how the building was viewed locally. Built on the edge of Bettws council estate, it was often referred to (in that most overused of architectural slurs) as an 'eyesore', and attracted an array of derogatory nicknames ranging from the severe (Colditz) to the more comic (Sausage Factory). It remains painfully ironic that a group of architects attracted to, as Reyner Banham suggests, a building being 'immemorially at home in its landscape setting' should find their own buildings (as in the case of Newport High School) sometimes rejected and vilified by the communities in which these buildings made their home.

Colditz and the Sausage Factory: the choice of these nicknames is revealing with regards to the attitudes adopted by the local community in relation to this building. It is likely that the popularity of the nickname, Colditz, can be traced back to the BBC television series of the same name that began broadcasting in 1972 (a year after the school was completed). Colditz is a nickname that is certainly not chosen for any architectural affinity with Brutalism. The once World War II prisoner-of-war camp is a many-times-renovated castle that contains aspects of the Gothic, an architectural style in binary opposition to Brutalism. What, then, was the connection? Did the residents of the estate think that the school looked like a prison? Did the pupils feel imprisoned inside of it? Perhaps it was the word itself that seemed fitting: *Cold-itz*. It has become a cliché to describe Modernist buildings as cold. But if one adds to this the quite violent sounding sibilance of the *t* and *z* – *itz* – the name *sounds* harsh in a way that might have felt congruent with the school's architecture However, any attempt to speculate about a connection between the nickname, Colditz, and the school's architecture is highly problematic, not least because there is at least one other school in Wales (whose design has no association with Brutalism) that also acquired the nickname, 'Colditz'. On the other hand, the second nickname, The Sausage Factory,[84] would seem to be a more peculiar choice, yet one similarly rich with implications. The factory can be seen as an emblem of capitalist exploitation: the monotonous antithesis of a creative and intrinsically satisfying labour. Further, the choice of sausage, slightly comic perhaps, is a food we might generally think of as cheap and mass-produced: the leftovers from the prime cuts of meat, squeezed into a uniform of synthetic intestinal sacks. To name this foodstuff as the factory's product is unlikely to be intended as a compliment to the school. To what extent this nickname (as with Colditz) is a response to the building itself rather than social and educational factors is, of course, debatable. However, to grow up in the learning environment suggested by these nicknames is perhaps not to grow up in an environment likely to facilitate a great sense of self-worth. As the social psychologist, Arnulf Kolsted, argues:

The perception of ourselves, who we are, depends partly on the environment that we are part of. We define ourselves as a constituent part of the environment, and if the environment has a high value or status, this value is transmitted to each individual who is a constituent part of this totality.[85]

Following this reasoning, if the environment was considered bleak or of low value, these characteristics would similarly be transmitted to its inhabitants. If we compare the implications of the nicknames (a cold, inhuman prison; a factory churning out sacks of scraps) with the ideals of the architects (a building at one with its environment, establishing an affinity with its inhabitants; wonderfully functional), a chasm begins to open up.

So why this chasm? The reasons are manifold and contestable (not least because of the aforementioned social and educational factors, as well as how the building is maintained and its facilities used) but for the purposes of this essay (as it pertains to the concerns of my poem), I will limit my discussion to two main points about the building and how it might be experienced. The first issue is seemingly simple and often remarked upon: the use of concrete. Banham writes that concrete 'under the hard glare of the Mediterranean sun gave something of the effect of [...] the apses of Michelangelo's St Peter's in Rome, on which Le Corbusier had written some of the most emotional prose in *Vers une Architecture*'. That is, it looked majestic and radiant. But as has often been noted, although concrete may take on this beatific appearance in the 'hard glare of the Mediterranean', the British climate with its many months of low grey skies provides a starkly different environment. Thus, British concrete structures can not only lack the 'St Peter's in Rome' effect, but can take on an appearance that some find at best dull and at worst strikingly ugly and forbidding.[86] So rather than people mentioning Michelangelo, we might hear talk of grim, concrete monoliths (Newport High School was sometimes referred to in this way).

The second of these issues (relating to the gulf between the ideals of the architect and the experience of the user) is more complex, as it concerns questions of aesthetics and taste. Arnulf Kolsted argues that the instinctive preferences we have as infants are, as we grow up, modified by individual experiences, but also by internalising the 'values and preferences in a particular society and culture'. [87] This process of internalising certain values would suggest that in any given culture there might be certain collective aesthetic passions and prejudices which would inform the designing of public or municipal buildings.[88] However, and this is where the chasm begins to open up, the aesthetic values absorbed by the general public can often be strikingly different to those absorbed by architects. Kolsted writes:

> Architects' preferences and tastes are normally different from lay people's, due to the same developmental principle explaining differences between infants and adults. Professionals have a broader experience and a deeper knowledge partly as a result of using other concepts and yardsticks.[89]

Consequently, what might seem impressive, even beautiful to an architect could quite possibly appear strange or distressing to a layperson, because these two groups of people are, in some respects, seeing with different eyes. This disparity between the view of the architect and that of the layperson is never more apparent and socially problematic than in the case of Brutalism. Not only does Brutalism rely on a material (concrete) that many (though not all) find unpleasing to the eye in a British environment, but much of its architectural vision is guided by an aesthetic (or ethic) that is mostly only well understood by those inside architectural and associated intellectual circles. Therefore, aspects of the building's structural harmony and circulation patterns might remain elusive to the majority of the building's users – hence the accusations of elitism.[90]

Henri Lefebvre, the French philosopher and theorist of space, would characterise this divide I've been writing of as the difference between *representations of space* and *spaces of representation*. *Representations of space* are 'conceptualized' spaces, the space of 'planners, urbanists, technocratic subdividers and social engineers'. It is 'the dominant space in any society'. The structure of Newport High School (conceived as it was by architects with stipulations from the local council) could be seen to fall into this category.[91] *Spaces of representation*, on the other hand, are *'lived'* spaces, 'the space of the "inhabitants" and "users", but also of some artists [...] This is the dominated – and hence passively experienced – space which the imagination seeks to change and appropriate.' In relation to the high school this would be primarily the experience of those who studied or worked there – the nicknames mentioned earlier could be considered attempts to 'change and appropriate' via the imagination. These spaces form two parts of Lefebvre's 'spatial triad'. The third component, *spatial practice*, relates to how space is perceived.

However, despite the delineations Lefebvre marks out, the philosopher stresses that these spaces do not easily separate: they overlap and interpenetrate. And it is this interpenetration I've tried to encourage in my poem about the school. Lefebvre makes the note that students of spaces of representation (like anthropologists and psychoanalysts, say) 'nearly always forget to set them alongside those representations of space which coexist, concord or interfere with them'.[92] However, 'the object of the exercise', from Lefebvre's point of view, 'is to rediscover the unity of the productive process'.[93] Therefore, it is as a form of spatial practice, wherein lived and conceived spaces are placed in a dialectical relationship in order to transform perception, that I see my poem operating.

I have attempted to do this via both the form and content of the poem (although as with Lefebvre's spaces there are no stable demarcations here; as Robert Creeley says: 'FORM IS NEVER MORE THAN AN EXTENSION OF CONTENT').[94] The poem is a sequence of short lyric fragments about the lived experience of the school's users juxtaposed with passages about the building itself – its construction and decay – and the theories that informed it. I set these alongside each other with an eye to destabilising the divide between the lived and conceived space. For example:

> *there was to be a set of specialist... areas for...*
> *domestic science and metalwork,*
> *which were seen as appropriate*
> *to the needs of the... area.*

Our first task is to make a bracelet
from a curl of copper.
                    Pushed deep
into the buffer wheel,
            each curl seeks

                    in that spinning
the colour of sunrise in January.

Here I have set some stipulations from the council to the architects about work areas, against a short lyric depicting an activity in one of those very work areas – a metalwork class. The conceived space and the lived space follow each other, hopefully informing each other: one is read or heard in light of the other.

A further feature of this extract is that the first half is a direct quotation (in this case from a report by the Twentieth Century Society).[95] There is a fair amount of this kind of 'found' poetry in the text – quotations from architects, commentators and an ex-student – that I have edited and arranged into lines. The rationale behind inserting these quotations into the text (beyond its apt congruence with 'Brutalism's preference for the "as found"'[96]) is suggested by the Objectivist poet George Oppen's, *Of Being Numerous*. The Oppen scholar Michael Davidson says that it is the use of 'extensive quotation from correspondence, conversations, books, and news articles [that] give vivid form [to what is] announced by the poem's title.'[97] The poem is concerned with 'unity in diversity, with achieving autonomy while living among others'.[98] 'We are pressed, pressed on each other',[99] Oppen writes, and the insertion of quotations in his work can be seen as attempts to reflect that social reality. Earlier in this essay I referred to the divide between the architects' taste and that of the laypeople's, between the planners' objectives and the lived experience, but there are also differing views within the community itself. The school might have often been maligned, but for those students who spent their formative years there it was also a storehouse of memories. Many were upset about its destruction. So one can see how the school attracts many varied and conflicting viewpoints. In consideration of this, I have chosen not to put forward just one speaker's subjective perspective on the matter within the poem, but have chosen, following Oppen, 'the meaning / Of being numerous';[100] I have attempted to create a polyvocal experience – a poem of many voices that aim to deepen and complicate one another. The poem opens with this (which acts as a kind of prelude):

> *It was a brilliant exposition*
> *of concrete construction, modular design*
> *and orderly planning.*
>
> The prize-winning structure was
> *Unloved and derided locally...seen*
> *as a liability... failing*
> *the area's children.*
>
> And here we come,

walking the tarmac lane into the grey container,
into the chasm
                            between one
version of the story and another.

Again I have used quotations (those words italicised), other
voices that offer different perspectives that don't so much oppose
each other, as see things from different angles. I then offer a
reflection in the final lines, which again refers to the lived
experience of the students. However, in many ways the students
in this fragment represent what the poem itself is trying to do.
The poem is trying to walk into this chasm, to explore the divide
between the *representations of space* and the *spaces of representation*
(between the conceived and the lived). And although when it
comes to the quotations in the poem, I choose whose voice gets
heard and when, and therefore the poem can never really be said
to remove itself from the shadow of my own prejudices, it does
aspire through acts of language and imagination to move toward
creating a spatial practice that might go some small way to
revealing how the space of Newport High School was/is
produced.

from THE BRUTALIST SCHOOL

It was a brilliant exposition
of concrete construction, modular design
and orderly planning.
                    The prize-winning structure was
Unloved and derided locally... seen
as a liability... failing
the area's children.
                    And here we come,
walking the tarmac lane into the grey container,

into the chasm
                    between one
version of the story and another.

    Grey javelins of rain
    slide off the diggers
    through spatters of mud.
    They move, guided not
    by beauty, but *Truth*
            to Materials:

girders of steel, caked in Forticrete
blocks rise up from the marshland.

there was to be a set of specialist… areas for…
domestic science and metalwork,
which were seen as appropriate
to the needs of the… area.

    Our first task is to make a bracelet
    from a curl of copper.
                    Pushed deep
    into the buffer wheel,
            each curl seeks
                    in that spinning
    the colour of sunrise in January.

The waffle slab ceilings arc above us
like a canopy of bathtubs, capsized.
We circulate through
            the gridiron system,

and hold the handrails
            like tubes of scaffolding
as we dip and rise among the steps.

My compass clamps a stub of pencil,
Escher print pinned to the store cupboard door—

          figures, dressed
          identically,
          walk endlessly,
          an impossible staircase.

          Teacher sits marking—
if there isn't much noise   she doesn't look up.
I lean over a page of geometry,
          rest my chin on a polyester sleeve.
Sound of scribbling, collective murmur,
          I look out through a wall of windows—

Roof water drains to the straightened stream,
the concrete canoe pool. The day the school opened,
Design magazine took photographs
of a young boy posing in a kayak.

They hailed the school *a minor, if slightly flawed,*
          masterpiece.
          Now the *water feature*
is a dank pond—no boating permitted.
And the outside teaching terraces?
I'm unsure if they were ever used.

July, sitting on hard steps, feeling the heat
through my shirt, the patio pools with light—

a brief glimpse of the ideal: concrete
under the Mediterranean sun,
the radiant apses of St Peter's—
in awe of Michelangelo, Le Corbusier wrote,
reflect for a moment on this thunderbolt.

The school is an outstanding example
of British modern architecture
... based upon a clear hierarchy
of ordered spaces... unique
in its architectural beauty
and intellectual rigour.

The Welsh sky grows low and heavy with cloud—
the building darkens with foreboding.

Algae spread over water, a swollen bin bag
floats in the feature   among flecks of waste.
An abandoned fridge—cord wriggling through
a mulch of leaves—lies beside the drain.
In a classroom held up columns, a sign:

This is a Positive Thinking area

Windows that looked down on the green-cork gym,
replaced by sets of steel plates. Metal-mesh
fences off the smokers' plateau. The slabs
are blackened with time. From ceilings stalactites ripple
and glisten. And yellow pansies, dwarfed
by their octagon pots, reach on thin stems
toward the thin light.

Diggers roll in   gouge out the classrooms.
Exposed: a tangle   of stiff steel veins.

Prints of memory   cling
to shattered slabs of concrete —

the bones of an ideal   worked into rubble.

I don't believe they should
have ever knocked it down.
It's like they have taken
a piece of my history away
and I know my friends feel the same.

All that remains now is water
and flattened plains of red mud,
       speckled with grey.

Two refugee geese are circling.

Bibliography

Banham, Reyner, *The New Brutalism* (London: The Architectural Press, 1966)

Bullock, Nicholas, 'Building the Socialist Dream or Housing the Socialist State? Design versus the Production of Housing in the 1960s', in *Neo-avant-garde and Postmodern: Postwar Architecture in Britain and Beyond*, ed. Mark Crinson and Claire Zimmerman (New Haven & London: Yale University Press, 2010)

Cold, Birgit, ed., *Aesthetics, Well-being and Health: Essays within architecture and environmental aesthetics*(Aldershot: Ashgate Publishers, 2001)

Davidson, Ian, *Ideas of Space in Contemporary Poetry* (Basingstoke: Palgrave, 2007)

Glancey, Jonathan, 'A great place to live'. Available at:

http://www.guardian.co.uk/education/2001/sep/07/arts.higher education [accessed 5/7/2010]

Hanley, Lynsey, *Estates: An Intimate History* (London: Granta, 2007)

Hatherley, Owen, *Militant Modernism* (Winchester: Zero Books, 2008)

Hoover, Paul, ed., *Postmodern American Poetry* (New York: Norton, 1994)

Lefebvre, Henri, *The Production of Space*, trans. Donald Nicholson-Smith (Oxford: Blackwell, 2009)

Merrifield, Andrew, *Henri Lefebvre: A Critical Introduction* (New York and London: Routledge, 2006)

Oppen, George, *New Collected Poems* (New York: New Directions, 2008)

Smithson, Alison & Peter, *Without Rhetoric: An Architectural Aesthetic 1955–1972* (London: Latimer New Directions, 1973)

Stevens Curl, James, 'Brutalism', in *A Dictionary of Architecture and Landscape Architecture* (2000). Available at: http://www.encyclopedia.com [accessed 15/3/2010]

Wright, Jon, 'Case Reports > Newport High School'. Available at: http://www.c20society.org.uk/casework/reports/2008/newport -high-school.html [accessed 8/6/2010]

Finding the Words: Using Found Text to Write the Human Impact of Environmental Disaster

Elizabeth-Jane Burnett

Writing urban space today is increasingly a task of environmental activism. This question of writing as activism can be usefully approached through Joan Retallack's figuring of the poethical wager. Retallack writes:

> The idea of the poethical "wager" is something that came to me during an "experimental barbecue" at my house with the poets Tina Darragh and Peter Inman. The conversation was, in part, about how we could choose to go on working in the culturally isolated field of experimental poetry when the whole world seemed to going to hell all around us. All three of us…had activist backgrounds…So the question arises…shouldn't we be devoting ourselves entirely to direct social action rather than the luxury of poetry? I think this is an intermittent question for many of us, and…I find it…a bracing one…my answer is poethical and certainly a form of "we don't know but we can try."[101]

Discussing the writing of the text in *When the Water Came: Evacuees of Hurricane Katrina (Interview-poems by Cynthia Hogue, Photographs by Rebecca Ross)* at the *Skylines* Ecopoetics forum in Devon where the work was showcased, Cynthia Hogue said that she did not know what type of language, other than documentary reportage, to use to describe the trauma of those living with the legacy of the hurricane.[102] She felt she did not have the right to speak on their behalf, or to mediate their words with her own emotional response, therefore found materials, interview transcripts and Rebecca Ross's photographs were her only possible materials.

However, mediation, and emotional response can figure in the way these found materials are employed. The poem for James Davidson (Figure 1) uses excerpts from an interview transcript with Davidson, but the visual placement of the words on the page, with shortening and lengthening lines, is Hogue's own method of commenting on her material. These undulating line lengths create a pattern of waves in tune with Davidson's sensation "of being in flood water over and over" (2). One large inward sweep from the line ending with "dreams" (1) down to "wake up" (11) conveys a sense of the moment transfixed, in an intermediary state between dreaming and waking, belief and disbelief, as the hurricane first takes hold of both the city and the onlookers' consciousness. With these line breaks, Hogue manages to comment on the words in the transcript without including her own words, and in this way constructs a relationship between author and subject in which the author figures more as sympathetic listener than direct speaker. The use of found materials in this way does not therefore aspire to complete objectivity, as the subjectivity of the author is still present but made secondary to that of the interviewee, whose words alone are featured.

Hogue's is a different approach to objectivity than that presented by news media coverage of environmental disaster. Speaking at the Bowery Poetry Club, New York, and also at the Kelly Writers House in Philadelphia, Anne Waldman critiqued the large scale euphemism adopted by media discourse, describing such coverage as operating through a system of "outrageous metaphor."[103] Waldman is another poet to whom the relationship between poetic practice and activism is important, as explored in *Outrider*[104], her 2007 poetic text that mixes found materials such as government reports and interview transcripts with more lyrical writing. After detailing how: "The U S of A is the single largest producer of greenhouse emissions generating twenty per cent of the global total... (and)...there is a kind of death wish in the land as a child in Africa dies of malaria every 30 seconds...the psychological suffering, in fact the "wounded psyche" all around is palpable," she then poses the important, capitalised question "WHAT IS THIS TO POETRY?"[105] Environmental and humanitarian disasters are linked in her questioning as she proceeds to describe how "the movies and media continue to glamorize war...you see the same computerised shot of the abstracted "other" over and over again...the oft-repeated degraded images of...people looting and pillaging - another example of the de-humanizing agenda of corporate-media-thug rule."[106] But how to humanize these issues without reducing them to banal pathos, tired images, phrases, and caricature is problematic.

Front door with trees, Jim's Louisiana home, New Orleans, Louisiana and Front steps, Jim's Louisiana home, New Orleans, Louisiana. Both images copyright Rebecca Ross, 2008.

James Davidson, Artist (excerpt)
Months before Katrina, I started having dreams
of being in flood water over and over.
They were not bad dreams, not scary,

but in each dream I was chest deep
in water making my way to an exit
or an entrance to higher ground.
A lot of people were helping
each other get together
up to higher ground so
there was no fear.
Then I'd wake up.
It never dawned on me
     my dreams were
          telling me something.
Our dreams are so peculiar.
The day we evacuated,
I didn't want to leave.
Bob said, *We have to get out of here.*
Yea, ok. *We've got to go.*
We drove to Memphis.
CNN showed people trying to get up
to the I-10 overpass and I said
(you don't want this on tape),
Fuck. I just don't believe it.
I'd had so many of those dreams
and then to see that water
     pouring into the city and all
         those people stuck there.

Figure 1: "James Davidson" from *When the Water Came: Evacuees of Hurricane Katrina*[107]

The use of images in poetic practice, and a consideration of the relationship between text and image, are factors that Hogue and Ross consider in their collaboration. The photographs Ross took of New Orleans were not predictable replications of flood-damaged areas or grief-stricken residents, but were instead images that held significance for the interviewees. They did not demand any immediate emotional response from the viewer but rather motivated them to engage in the process of establishing links between interviewee and accompanying image, and through this process learning more about the person interviewed, and what New Orleans meant to them personally. Size of image also played a part in the curation of this piece at the *Skylines* exhibition, as images, so often the predominant method of speaking of environmental disaster in the news media, are scaled-down in size, to be the same size, or smaller, than the accompanying text. The viewer is encouraged to look further than the image at hand, referring to the text in equal measure, with increased opportunities for asking questions about the relationship of image to text and of the role of the spectator in this, too often passive, viewing process. As Waldman states:

> I've always been interested in the role of the spectator. Where, how, why do we actually engage in what it is we see? What is the provocation toward engagement or action. Of course the artist is always engaged. One is both the spectator and the spectacle as the artist. Or rather, the work is the spectacle. Witness involves being there to testify...But when millions of people watching television see abandoned citizens on rooftops begging for water that doesn't arrive for 4-5 days, what do they do?...What can one do?...It's an endless struggle. And a fragile one. You have to uncover the extremities - of the collateral damage...because it's not being "shown" to us."[108]

As Waldman recounts, news media either represents issues by the mass duplication of increasingly stultifying images, or entirely neglects to cover them. In Hogue's text, it is perhaps possible to read a frustration at the limitations of this type of reporting in the lines:

> CNN showed people trying to get up
> to the I-10 overpass and I said
> (you don't want this on tape) (21-23)

The media-relayed image of people evacuating is conflicted by the line "you don't want this on tape" (23) - a censorship is hinted at, a sense of what constitutes an appropriate image for recording. It is then followed by a registering of disbelief, and the suggestion that what is being viewed might be fictitious - "I'd had so many of those dreams" (25) - the media portrayal of these events becomes dreamlike, with the all too familiar images of grief and disaster no longer registering on any real, personal, level. Hogue's poem suggests a fuller portrayal of events, as she is able to include bracketed text, thoughts that might otherwise be censored, aspects that perhaps "you don't want...on tape" (23). Similarly in the next poem, "Catherine Loomis, Professor," Loomis recalls how:

> Friday, I was at Sally's house watching CNN,
> and we said, *That storm moved.*
> On the way home, I bought all the water left
> at Save-a-Center, and when I saw the display
> of batteries at the front, I thought,
> I ought to get a pack. That small decision
> saved my life. Sunday the sky turned
> an awful orange. (3-10)

It is the mix of media reportage through an individual's eyes -"I was at Sally's house watching CNN" (3), with incidental detail "I saw the display/ of batteries at the front, I thought, I ought to get a pack. That small decision/ saved my life" (6-9), and lyrical imagery where "the sky turned/an awful orange" (9-10) that enables a fuller picture of events to be presented here; with the possibility of registering emotively, and visualising scenes beyond the manufactured, mass produced, and therefore to an extent expected, images of grief or disaster presented by CNN. Waldman discusses the importance of placing the individual in issues of environmental and humanitarian disaster, and partly enables this by relating both issues to the human body. In *Outrider* she articulates a link between the human body, the body politic, and the landscape of the natural world, asking:

> What is a poetics of body speech and mind in a charnel ground of corpses who rise up once again to say "never again?" We need witness collectives...never again, this madness against the body, OUTRIDER citizens, not again.[109]

She offers a sense of poetry's role as vigilant witness to bodily, political and environmental stress, to trespass and atrocity, and to the need to question how poetry can articulate this vigilance, and document this history of accumulating trauma. And not just to document, but to document with compassion and urgency. She also presents the archive as a method of witness, as, extending further into the political, she expresses an urgent need to record humanitarian and environmental tragedies, to act as evidence or as warnings to future generations:

> Will generations hence look back at this time and see it as another Holocaust where we didn't take care of each other or our world? Where poets might have accomplished more in the area of human rights, in alleviating the suffering of the poor and impoverished...
> As of this writing 55,000 dead in Pakistan, the toll rising.
> Three million people without shelter.[110]

Statistics, dates, and quoted speech run through *Outrider*, as Waldman echoes in her textual practice, the running of the renowned tape and digitised archive at Naropa. She reels off facts and figures: "Nearly 400 billion in the Pentagon budget" (43), "plutonium leaked into the soil remain a danger as of October, 2005" (48), and describes using in her writing: "a little report on one of the workers in the aftermath of ground zero in November 2001" (42). She concludes that:

> We need to investigate and document relevant information and stay on it...work with like-minded compassionate warriors of Change.[111]

Waldman's language here is bellicose, as she voices not only a poetic motivation to write of environmental disaster, but a religious one too. This faith helps explain the paradox in being conceived of as a warrior of compassion, as Waldman's response to activism is tempered by a spiritual drive to convert the need for environmental and humanitarian aid to peaceful poetic protest on the page, and to peaceful political protest on the streets and in the courts. Waldman's Buddhist faith is one that Hogue shares, and guided Waldman in the building of a poetics school at Naropa, Colorado. These Buddhist beliefs were at the heart of Naropa's inception, as Waldman writes:

> The Boddhisattva Vow involves a practice of *tonglen*, or sending and receiving practice in which the practitioner takes on - visually, emotionally - the suffering of others. Allen Ginsberg spoke of this time (late 20th century) being a time of grieving, and of "trying the human" - "everything else/drunken dumb show"...an acute sense of the larger picture was/is always present.[112]

This is not to suggest that the religious dimension of either Waldman or Hogue's practice is central to a reading of its functioning as environmental activism however, as without these religious insights the issues of how to write environmental disaster with a human aspect or compassionate awareness that manages to avoid Waldman's "outrageous metaphor" remain.

Cecilia Vicuña's urban installations employing "precario" - small, ephemeral structures made from debris and found objects - provide another method of challenging news media's often de-personalised methods of communication. Jena Osman, in her article "Is Poetry the News"[113] compares Vicuña's precario with the billboard artwork of Alfredo Jarr. Jarr's artwork, placed in public spaces usually reserved for advertising, is large-scale, and offers a striking counterpoint to the fragility of Vicuña's work, exploring her dictum that "maximum fragility" can work against "maximum power", with power here being that accorded to the news media's methods of communication and representation. *Glass of Milk* (Figure 2) provides a particularly striking image to draw attention to the fact that over a thousand children in Bogota were dying each year from contaminated milk, without any action being taken against the distributors. Images of the spilled milk were made into street posters, inhabiting the same space as Jarr, and of standard news media, yet using it very differently. The piece was in the first instance a performance, an action performed in the street in Bogota, for which the images provide documentation, but in her use of small materials - a bottle of milk, spilled by her own hand - occupying a large media space that had not previously taken any notice of this issue, Vicuña offers a kind of documentation with compassionate awareness, such as Waldman or Hogue might prescribe.

In Redell Olsen's *Era of Heroes*,[114] a list of names (an excerpt from which is provided in Figure 3) provides the documentation of an action she performed in the street in London. Wearing Mickey Mouse Ears, Olsen walked in circles around the Bookartbookshop in Pitfield Street, reading continuously from a list of contemporary heroes and superheroes compiled in part from searches on the internet. Her voice was relayed into the bookshop and the audience could choose whether to stand in the street and watch her pass, or to listen to her voice from inside the shop. In the shop window a neon sign alternated between reading "eraofheroes" and "heroesoferror." Performed at a time when the U.S administration had declared a war on terror, with stereotypes of good and evil abounding, Olsen's list of superhero names enabled a critique of the type of maximum power that Vicuña operates against, and of this power's propensity for creating easily identifiable and either sympathetic or demonized characters for political purposes and perpetuating these images through the mass media. Olsen's list is itself an example of the "outrageous metaphor" Waldman speaks about, but taken to such an extreme as to comment on its own absurdity. The neon sign that also operated alongside this performance hints at the way that the viewer might question these images of heroism perpetuated in the media, switching as it does between spelling the official "era of heroes" and the more anarchically phrased "heroes of errors."

Figure 2: Cecilia Vicuña, *Glass of Milk*[115]

Marvel Bunny, Marvelo, Marvex the Suber-Robot, Marvo the Magician, Mary Marvel, Mask, Masked Marvel (I) & (II), Masked Ranger, Masked Rider, Master Key, Masterman, Master Mind Exello, Mekano, Menta, Merciless the Sorceress, Mercury, Merlin, Merry the Girl of 1000 Gimmicks, Merzah the Mystic, Meteor, Mickey, Mickey Martin, Micro

Figure 3: Redell Olsen from *Era of Heroes*[116]

In these diverse poetic practices interacting with different urban spaces, it is in the handling of found materials that an affective and activist response to the environmental and humanitarian issues currently at stake is played out. Retallack's question of "how we could choose to go on working in the culturally isolated field of experimental poetry when the whole world seemed to be going to hell all around us"[117] is answered by diverse religious, political, and aesthetic motivations, but common to all the practices discussed here is an attempt at making these issues personal to the reader or viewer in a way that mass media is often unable to do. Whether it is the use of personal testimony and incidental detail as in Hogue's poems in *When the Water Came: Evacuees of Hurricane Katrina,* or the use of small, everyday items like milk bottles in Vicuña's precario pieces, or by individual action, as with Olsen's solitary, costumed walk through London in *Era of Heroes,* issues and events are drawn attention to in ways it is difficult to observe passively. In "Victoria Green, Mother of Four," another of the interview-poems from *When the Water Came: Evacuees of Hurricane Katrina,* Green states:

> These times you remember every kid
> you went to first grade with
> by *name.* You wonder where
> *everybody* was, the bum
> on the corner, the pickpocketers,
> the little man that's always on Bourbon Street
> painting the city. CNN was showing people on houses.
> This was not a strange neighborhood to me.
> This was *my* neighborhood…
> You'd have to be a citizen
> of New Orleans to understand.[118]

Through using the voices of New Orleans citizens Hogue goes

some way towards making us understand. Poetry can offer ways of writing environmental disaster that provide more opportunities for personal engagement than the mass media often can, and through doing so, can be viewed as having an important role to play in an environmental context. How far-reaching the effects of this role can, or will, be is impossible to say. Can writing poems ever be enough? In the end, like Retallack, "my answer is poethical and...a form of "we don't know but we can try."" [119]

Bibliography

Garrard, Greg. *Ecocriticism*. New York: Routledge, 2004.
Hogue, Cynthia. *Or Consequence*. Pasadena, CA: Red Hen Press, 2010.

—-.*The Incognito Body*. Los Angeles: Red Hen Press, 2006.
Ijima, Branda, ed. *((eco(lang) (uage (reader))*. Brooklyn, N.Y.: Portable Press at Yo-Yo Labs; Callicoon, N.Y: Nightboat Books, 2010.

Olsen, Redell. *Secure Portable Space*, Reality Street Editions, 2004.
Osman, Jena, "Is Poetry the News?: Poethics of the Found Text", Jacket, 32, 2007

Retallack, Joan. *The Poethical Wager*. University of California Press, 2002.

Vicuña, Cecilia. *Instan*. Berkeley, California: Kelsey Street Press, 2002

Waldman, *Outrider, Essays, Interview, Poems*. Albuquerque: La Alameda Press/ University of New Mexico, 2006.

—-. *Structure of the World Compared to a Bubble*. London: Penguin Poets, 2004.

—-. *Vow to Poetry: Essays, Interviews, & Manifestos*. Minneapolis: Coffee House Press, 2001.

Urban Space as a Collection of Poetry

Jan Hatt-Olsen

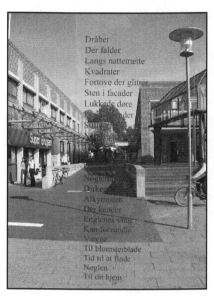 

The pictures above are from a poetry-installation / public art project, which was a cooperation between myself, the people of downtown Værløse, and the local business life. Værløse is a town with 18000 inhabitants, in Furesø Municipality in the Greater Copenhagen area. Downtown Værløse was transformed into a collection of poetry from 3 September – 12 September 2004 by the installation of 61 new poems by myself, printed on 61 transparent Plexiglas plates (2 m x 0.3 m). These plates were placed on pillars and walls, hung from trees, and stood in large pots filled with soil (as small 'poetry trees') in every public square in the area. I also installed 4 'poetry roads' (with a length of a little over 1 km), constructed of 141 stickers (1m x 0.3 m) pasted to the grounds of public squares and streets. Each road was a poem and each sticker contained one line of that poem.

The stickers of poetry were placed at regular intervals so each road would have its own visual rhythm.

Downtown Værløse as a Collection of Poetry was published by the experimental Danish publisher Tiara. The ISBN number, title and author were printed on one of the Plexiglas plates and placed on the second pillar in the main square in order to be seen by those arriving at the local train station. The idea behind this was to facilitate a recognition that urban spaces are like collections of poems. Urban spaces – like squares, roads, parks, gardens, bridges, neighborhoods or whole cities – are condensed human imagination, in both material and spiritual form, where narratives and well-structured syntax can be found (although this is a fragmented world of imagination with no *unifying* narrative). As a book of poetry is registered with the international standard book number, so too are the urban spaces along a transport system in a well-organized city – each space is named, registered and mapped in official systems.

Furthermore, you are able to view poetry in urban spaces in an often surprisingly similar manner to the way you view a codex book or the scroll. The scroll, for instance, is a two dimensional space, with one dominant dimension and two main directions – the scroll is like a road. One of the comments I got when I was taking photos of the installation was from a girl who told me that she really liked to bike through the main road early in the morning, because when she biked the lines on the 'poetry road' would meet her eyes one line after another (as she passed each sticker of text). She was reading the road like a scroll.

However, unlike a book or a scroll, when urban space becomes a collection of poetry, anyone and anything can and do contribute to that poetry, anyone is a poet, and anything in the city can become part of several poems. It is a collection of poetry which is both physical and spiritual; that is, the physical buildings are registered and yet the installation is also an act of the imagination, something that cannot be registered in any system (which is also the case in any book of poetry). But the objective of the installation is not really to *transform* urban space into a collection of poetry, but rather for the installation to act as a catalyst that enables people to see that urban space is *already* a collection of poetry, in which everybody is both reader and writer.

People moving through the installation would see the shadows and reflections of the words all around them. As the wind moved the transparent Plexiglas plates that hung down from trees –as if floating in the air – and the sun moved the shadows of words during the day it created a flux of spaces and words; a flux of poetized urban space. As the area of the installation included the town hall, post office, cinema, library, culture house, coffee shops, police station, as well as almost all the shops in the city, a park and some residential areas, there were always people living in this collection of poetry, this poetized urban space. This was a collection of poetry that was constantly changing, constantly being rewritten by the way people moved through, used or related to the urban space and each other, as well as by the way the wind and sun impacted on the Plexiglas plates.

Often this rewriting was very deliberate. In the photo overleaf (Figure 1.) can be seen a sticker pasted on a red brick ground (the main square in the area is actually called the red square). The sticker is part of a 'poetry road' from the city hall to the culture house. Translated in to English, the words printed on it read, 'something is being broken' or 'which is broken'. However, a passer by has pasted on to the large sticker a new, smaller yellow sticker, with the text: 'it is prohibited to paste'. Other examples of this kind of interaction were that people would make sticks with small papers on them printed with a few words and plant the sticks in the pots of soil next to the 'poetry trees' so that they looked like new smaller trees growing up around them (see

Figure 1.   Figure 2.

Figure 2.). To add your own tagged work to that of others' work is a part of what is accepted in the rules of street art, and the same approach works here, creating a play of poetry in downtown Værløse.[120]

The purpose of the installation/intervention was to highlight my idea that urban space is text, that visual poetry and written poetry are essentially the same: both are poetized spaces in flux, created and re-created by writing and reading, regulated by editors and publishers or by planners and politicians, analyzed and commented on by critics or urbanists, and, of course, the public. I wanted to draw attention to the possibility of a poetic reality which has no separation between text, context and media; a hyper complex reality you can live in, leave or enter (which at the same time can be a Chôra, a space in-between, always being created) where even the smallest scratch in a wall, a person walking down a street, or a written word is a gateway to poetical transcendence.

William Blake is a strong source of inspiration for this work. In his illuminated books, he developed a synthesis of visual art and poetry that aims to express a world where everything has meaning. His art attempted to shift the reader's/viewer's perception of the world, to enable them to see it as it really is:

If the doors perception were cleansed
every thing would appear to man as it is.
Infinite
For man has closed himself up, till he sees
All things thro' the narrow chinks of his cavern.[121]

An illuminated book of Blake's is not just part of a three dimensional world, but is also part of an infinite world. Blake describes infinity thus:

The nature of infinity is this: That everything has its
Own Vortex, and when once a traveler thro' Eternity
Has passed that Vortex he perceives it roll backward behind
His path, into a Globe itself infolding : like a Sun :
Or like a moon or like a Universe of starry majesty,
While he keep onwards his wondrous journey on the earth,
Or like a human form, a friend [with] whom he livd
    benevolent.[122]

I share with Blake the idea of a work of art as a process, an eternal journey (so long as there is a world of imaginations it can travel through) and I think the same is true for the city. The city is a process, it is a journey through the world of the imaginations of all those who live in it, use it or think of it. I do not fully share Blake's antirealism though;[123] there is a world out there, but it is a world that can be fused with imaginations to create an augmented reality in a way never seen before. And this can be aided by the kind of techniques employed in the installation.

Blake insists that he sees everything in the world as in his illuminated books, and what is so special about our time is that we can take Blake's philosophy and confront it with the reality of the city: its social dynamics and its physical infrastructure and architecture; we can combine Blake's cosmos with urban planning; we can change the perception of the city and the ontology of urban space. And this can be, at least partly, achieved by the kind of poetry installation/intervention discussed in this essay. However, it is important that this kind of installation isn't just public art / poetry, but links with urban planning and archi-tecture and includes all the inhabitants of the area or neigh-borhood, so people take part in it and use or misuse it in their daily life, just as they would any other urban space. This process involves a close collaboration with the urban planners of the city, the municipality, the local commerce and the citizens. The idea is that when the art / literature / urban plan, *Urban Space as a Collection of Poetry* is installed, its animating and poetizing effects will not be confined to the virtual, the private, the inner space, but will transform all objects and persons in the physical public space into poets and poetry itself. Ultimately this will lead to Urban Space being perceived to be the collection of poetry it already is, regardless of the stickers and Plexiglas. This change of perception will change the urban space to an urban place, and the significance of this change from space to place will be charac-terized by the creation of meaning. A place in which we can physically and mentally stop and where we experience stories being created; a place to tell stories about, to others and ourselves. And as the art historian, Nicoletta Isar commented on the place that has been the subject of this essay:

The city of Værløse miraculously became the city of words of poetry – *Alphaville* – a place of wonder where man poetically dwells.[124]

Bibliography

Blake, William, *William Blake: The Complete Illuminated Books*, introduction David Bindman, London: Thames and Hudson, 2000.

Hatt-Olsen, Jan. *Værløse Bymidte den. 3 Sept. – 12 Sept. 2004 | Lyrik-installation / Bog / Digtsamling*, Copenhagen: Tiara 2004.

Hatt-Olsen, Jan. *Værløse Bymidte den. 3 Sept. – 12 Sept. 2004 | Lyrik-installation / Bog / Digtsamling*. Available at: www.lyrik-installation.dk/Vaerloese [Accessed: June 25th 2010] 2004 – 2010.

Hatt-Olsen, Jan. *The City as an Expression of Poetry*, in Wayne McCready, ed. *Western Humanities Review, Fall 2007, Western Humanities Alliance Special Issue: Whats is a City,*

Salt Lake City: University of Utah, 2007. pp. 88-99.

Isar, Nicoletta. *Vision and Performance. A Hierotopic Approach to Contemporary Art,) Hierotopy Comparative Studies,* ed. Lidov, Alexei. Moscow: Indrik, 2009, pp. 328 – 362.

"That time at St. George's": Abandonment, Affect and Spatial Agency in two novels by Nicholas Royle

Holly Prescott

Come home with me to Greater Manchester for the summer holidays and there are things I cannot show you. I can't give you that satisfying yet slightly self-indulgent tour that maps out one's early life: 'here is where I was born'; 'here is where I first went to school', and the like. The reason I cannot do this is because physically—materially—these autobiographically significant buildings no longer exist. The local maternity hospital in which I was born closed in 2004, and in 2007 demolition work commenced in order to make way for a new housing venture. Furthermore, what was my infant school building is now home to a car park and sports pitches, while a large roundabout now stands on the old site of my junior school. It seemed as if the sites around which stories of my early life should grow, emanate and cross-pollinate were being erased from the local landscape. The more I thought about this, the more I felt compelled to seek some means of recovering the places of my infanthood from the amnesic void into which they seemed to have been resigned. So, I turned to that entity which has these days become synonymous with the very word 'search', and typed into Google the name of the now-defunct maternity unit in which I had been delivered. To my astonishment, the search results delivered back to me teemed with images of the hospital shortly after its doors closed, in a melancholy state of abandonment: wards and beds and medical equipment were all captured, lying dormant in limbo between the building's closure and its repossession. Practitioners of 'urban exploration', a 'weird hobby' which 'consists of seeking out, visiting and documenting interesting human-made spaces, most typically abandoned buildings'[125] had gained entry to the disused hospital and had done just that: they had photographically documented this birth-place that was no more. The maternity hospital in which I was born had therefore not disappeared at all, nor had it been forgotten—it had merely been uploaded, existing in photographic form on the web, for all internet users to explore, muse over and resurrect the narratives of their early lives.

It was through finding these online urban exploration photographs that I became fascinated with abandoned spaces, and became sensitized to what seemed to be a proliferation of discarded or derelict sites in contemporary literature and culture. I wanted to know why a surprising number of contemporary British authors, like the urban exploration photographers I'd found online, seemed to display something of a preoccupation with abandoned urban spaces, visiting and revisiting them in their prose narratives and, in places, deploying these disused or redeveloped spaces as the very catalysts for narrative itself. These spaces didn't seem to be merely passive scenery against which to set fictional action, but something much, much more. Indeed, my readings seemed to concur with Steve Pile's claim that stories are often '"produced" out of the spatialities that *seemingly only provide the backdrop* for those stories'[126] (my italics). In this essay therefore, I will focus specifically upon two novels by Cheshire-born author Nicholas Royle, *The Matter of the Heart* and *The Director's Cut*, in order to investigate some of the ways in which Royle in particular explores this notion of the abandoned urban space as a stimulus for narrative. In doing so, I will argue that it is difficult to read these spaces through the frameworks of much existing spatial theory, since authors like Royle present disused and redeveloped spaces as taking on something of an agency of their own, above and beyond human actualization, or being 'lived out' by human subjects: a concept for which much existing spatial theory leaves little analytical room.

Spatial Theory and the notion of 'Human Actualization'

As well as being staggered by this apparent contemporary preoccupation with abandoned spaces, I was also somewhat taken aback by a trend which seemed to have taken shape in much theoretical work accounting for the ways in which space—particularly urban space—is conceptualized and 'produced'. So much of the theory I read gave overwhelming emphasis to *human agency* in the production of urban space: that is to say, they reiterated the idea that 'space' is something produced principally through human action, or through humans 'living out' certain spaces through the repetition of social practices. For example, in *The Practice of Everyday Life*, Michel de Certeau famously describes space as *'practiced place'*, arguing that inert 'places' become socially-invested 'spaces' when they are brought to life, so to speak, through human actualization, such that 'the street geometrically defined by urban planning is transformed into a space by walkers'[127]

This accentuation of the role played by human agency in the production of urban space continues through many Marxist, material-historicist spatial theories like that of Henri Lefebvre, which emphasises space as a social product, and views the 'production of the city' as reliant upon 'the production of human beings by human beings'.[128] Lefebvre's seminal work *The Production of Space* takes as its springboard the idea that Western philosophy has, over time, reduced the concept of 'space' either to an empty container, subordinate to whatever 'fills' it, or to a purely mental or ideational category: space as mental, not physical or concrete. Space then, Lefebvre claimed, had become *fetishized* and had come to obfuscate the means of its own production. 'Instead of uncovering the social relationships [...] that are latent in spaces' Lefebvre argues, 'we fall into the trap of treating space as space "in itself", as space as such,' meaning that we come to 'fetishize space in a way reminiscent of the old fetishism of commodities'.[129] To address and correct this fetishization then, Lefebvre affirms that rather than just being a mysterious, vacuous 'thing', *'(social) space is a (social) product'*,[130] 'product' being 'the result of repetitive acts and gestures'.[131] This assertion may sound very familiar now, but wasn't quite so taken-for-granted in the intellectual climate against which Lefebvre composed *The Production of Space* (written in 1974). As with de Certeau however, Lefebvre's thought grants space-making agency to the social human being: 'social space' is produced as it is lived out through the repeated behaviours of a society's human population. Furthermore, as will prove crucial later in this discussion, Lefebvre's heavy Marxist influences means that he portrays this production of space in any given society as inextricably linked to the dominant modes and relations of production in that society. Consequently for Lefebvre, every society produces its own space: 'I say each society,' Lefebvre reflects, 'but it would be more accurate to say each mode of production, along with its specific relations of production'.[132] In rudimentary terms then, we might say that Feudalism, industrialism and capitalism are all based upon and reproduce certain distinct dominant modes and relations of production, and so hence all produce their own, distinct set of spatial organisations and relations.

What became more surprising however was the fact that even the contemporary scholarship which I discovered — scholarship portraying urban space as potentially playful and subversive — still often seemed to inherit this emphasis upon human agency in the 'production' of urban space. For example, Franck and Stevens's volume *Loose Space: Possibility and Diversity in Urban Life* discusses 'loose spaces', which are depicted as threshold urban spaces which come to be re-appropriated for purposes other then those for which they were intended. So, for example, city squares used by buskers and dancers, or steps outside a building that are re-appropriated by skateboarders as courses and obstacles could both be described as 'loose' spaces. Once again however, Franck and Stevens maintain that it is through human actualization that spaces become loose: 'many urban spaces possess [...] possibilities for looseness [...], but it is *people*, through their own initiative, who fulfil these possibilities' (my italics). Throughout their account, powerful and active verbs are attributed to humans and human agency, leaving the urban spaces themselves as merely 'open' to human appropriation: 'giving' or 'offering' human subjects the opportunity to 'create loose space'.[133] Characterising urban space as 'practiced place' then (de Certeau), as a 'social product' (Lefebvre) or as something fulfilled through human action and actualization (Franck & Stevens), overwhelmingly attributes the agency to 'produce' space to the social human being.

In coming to look closely at Nicholas Royle's fiction, I had two main issues with the above. Firstly came Lefebvre's idea that a certain society's space is both a product of, and at the same time works to perpetuate, the dominant modes and relations of production in that society. It therefore struck me that abandoned spaces lie *outside of, or have been left behind by* these dominant modes of production. Lefebvre's spatial scheme therefore seemed somehow lacking, as a problem thus presented itself as to how one might theoretically account for these obsolete, non-productive spaces, and their increasing appearance in contemporary fiction. Secondly, of course, came the issue of agency in the production of and conceptualisation of urban space. In the theories outlined above, the ability to act, cause or influence seemed to lie overwhelmingly with humans, with no room for exploring an idea which is central to my work: namely that space might have a power and agency of its own, and can operate above and beyond mere human actualization. I want to argue then that these issues are actually crucial to the ways in which Royle deploys abandoned spaces in his novels, so to perform a Lefebvrean reading of them would be an insufficient means of getting to the bottom of how and why abandoned spaces resonate through so much contemporary British writing.

The fiction of Nicholas Royle: *The Matter of the Heart*

Initially a short story writer with a passion for horror, Nicholas Royle[134] has gone on to publish five novels and one novella, as well as editing a number of short story collections including, *The Time Out Book of New York Short Stories* and *The Time Out Book of London Short Stories, Volume Two*. As the above titles suggest, Royle's fiction has a strong urban focus. He admits to having been influenced by Iain Sinclair, the eminent British psychogeographer whose work gave Royle the 'confidence' to pursue his urban themes, most significantly encouraging him to explore 'the way you can map a character's emotion into London locations'.[135] Crucial for this discussion however is the fact that Royle's novels expand upon a distinct preoccupation which resonates throughout much of his short-story writing: namely, a persistent focus upon *abandoned urban spaces*. 'I've always been obsessed with abandoned institutions, particularly abandoned hospitals and one hospital in particular, the one at Hyde Park Corner which used to be St George's Hospital' admits Royle,[136] and in his first novel *Counterparts*, Royle introduces St George's into his work as central character Gargan, a tightrope walker, discovers the abandoned hospital as a suitably covert and subversive site in which to attach his ropes and embark upon a high-wire walk above Hyde Park Corner.[137] In *The Matter of the Heart* however, St. George's plays a much more central role. The novel is centred upon an event which takes place within a certain room in the aforementioned abandoned hospital. Through stories told by secondary character Max, to the narrator of the novel, Chris we learn of an instance in which Max's elusive friend Danny sneaks into the abandoned hospital and has sex with his girlfriend 'Z' in the room in question. However, the text is replete with hints that 'something else' happened in that room that night, and only as the novel reaches its dénouement does the reader learn, through the technique of flashback or *analepsis*, that Danny and 'Z' are caught *in flagrante* by a security guard, who ties Danny up and rapes 'Z' right before him. Danny escapes and murders the security guard with a blow to the head, disposing of the body in the disused hospital's incinerator.

Royle spins a gruesome tale, an *homage* to his earlier fixation upon the horror genre. Nevertheless, what is most crucial for the purposes of this discussion is the way in which this derelict room in the abandoned hospital, introduced early in the very first chapter of the book, is then made to circulate and saturate the novel's narrative. After learning of Danny's sex-act, the reader is then presented with a fictional-historical urban legend, claiming that over one hundred years before Danny and Z's exploits, this particular room in St. George's was used by a certain crazed Dr. Maddox for a failed attempt at the world's first heart transplant. Furthermore, years later when the hospital is turned into a hotel, another friend of Max's, Charlie, suffers a massive heart attack while making love to his partner Yvonne in what transpires to be the site of the very same room: 'of course,' proclaims Chris, 'the room Yvonne and Charlie had in the fancy hotel was the same room used by Danny and Z all those years before'.[138] Royle's use of the phrase 'of course' here implies inevitability, suggesting that rather than existing as a mere 'product' (or waste-product) or 'creation' of human social relations and interactions as Lefebvre or Franck & Stevens might in their own schemes envision, the abandoned hospital itself actually exerts a power and agency of its own, able to determine the fate of the novel's human characters.

From here on in, the abandoned hospital haunts Royle's text, fuelling the narrative flow, and working to create feelings of suspense which again pay homage to Royle's fervour for horror stories. Even when narrator Chris visits Charlie in America, the hospital follows him across time and space, bubbling to the surface of the narrative as Charlie insists, 'That hospital, that room [...] It's some kind of place'.[139] Even as Chris moves on to Australia with his girlfriend Joanna, he has flashbacks of Max taunting that 'perhaps [...] you don't know as much about that night [in the abandoned hospital] as you think you do'[140] and, learning that Danny is now in Australia too, Chris is constantly vexed by thoughts such as 'whether the night in the abandoned hospital had affected his [Danny's] mind'.[141] Then suddenly, Chris's girlfriend is kidnapped, leading him on a vast search of the desolate Australian bushland in which he desperately tries to track Joanna down. The narrative agency behind his quest however turns yet again to be none other than the abandoned hospital, since the reader discovers that it is Danny who has kidnapped Joanna, as a result of 'her knowledge of what had happened that time at St. George's',[142] and that since his ill-fated visit to St. George's, Danny has in fact murdered Z, since their shared experience inside the abandoned hospital and her witnessing of Danny's murder of the security guard meant that 'she knew too much'.[143]

Royle's Abandoned Spaces and the notion of 'Affect'

Using the abandoned space as a narrative device, Royle explores a possibility not entertained by Lefebvre and the other theorists discussed earlier: namely, that space—particularly abandoned urban space—might somehow possess something of its own agency. Royle embeds the abandoned hospital into his text as an undercurrent: a latency constantly threatening to be made manifest, and driving the narrative along. Consequently, I want to argue that Royle's use of the abandoned hospital in *The Matter of the Heart* can be accounted for not in terms of the human production or actualization of urban space as the likes of de Certeau, Lefebvre and Franck & Stevens emphasise. Instead, I propose that Royle's deployment of the disused and then redeveloped hospital can be explored instead in terms of *affect*: a notion which explores emotional life, originating from a branch of psychoanalysis known as affect theory. As Ben Anderson explains, unlike emotion (with which it is often conflated), affect exists *transhumanly*: that is, rather than being tied to individual, discrete human subjects, affect is, as Hayden Lorimer describes, 'distributed between, and can happen outside, bodies which are not exclusively human, and might incorporate technologies, things, non-human living matter'.[144] Anderson thus describes affect as a 'context', a 'ceaselessly oscillating foreground/ background, or, better, an immanent "plane"'. When this 'plane' is actualized through the individual subject then a manifest emotion is produced. Rudimentarily then, emotion equals the actualization of affect, or of this transhuman affective field which Anderson describes. However, as well as these manifestations, Anderson says, 'Movements of affect are always accompanied by a real but virtual knot of tendencies and *latencies* that generate differences and divergences in what becomes real'.[145] Even when not actualized as perceivable emotions then, affective fields still very much exist, and still have the agency to influence the manifest world. It is here, therefore, that we come to the crucial link to Royle's use of the abandoned St. George's hospital. I propose that Anderson's characterisation of affect very closely echoes the way in which the defunct hospital works in *The Matter of the Heart*: Royle writes the hospital into the text as precisely such a 'plane', sometimes actualized within the consciousness of the characters; at other times lurking beneath and around the text, generating movements and channels of characters' thoughts, associations and (ultimately) action.

A Second Case: *The Director's Cut*

The above concept is far from exclusive to *The Matter of the* Heart. A very similar thing happens in Royle's later novel *The Director's Cut*, which begins at a demolition site on Tottenham Court Road, as a collection of older buildings are bulldozed to make way for a new complex. In the demolition however, the body of man, wrapped in celluloid film, is discovered within the remains of an abandoned cinema. As it transpires, the reader discovers that fifteen years before the novel is set in 1998, its four main characters—all film enthusiasts—made a film of a man committing suicide: a desperate man called Iain Burns, condemned to a slow death through tertiary syphilis. Once more therefore, like the hospital in *The Matter of the Heart*, the abandoned cinema and the secrets it conceals work as an initial catalyst for Royle's narrative. The defunct cinema space persists in haunting the characters throughout the novel, the abandoned space once again moving across and through the text, which, with its jumbled chronology darting back and forth from past to present, temporally, memorially and affectively persists in contracting back to that evening in the disused picture house. Most crucially however, echoing throughout *The Director's Cut* is the apparently most psychologically vulnerable character, Angelo's, obsession with abandoned and redeveloped cinemas. Before the making of his grim snuff movie, Iain Burns educates Angelo in the way of the disused movie theatre: 'this is where the love affair is consummated. Between you and what's on the screen, and in the air all around you. Believe me, this place and others like it- they're the ones that have the power. They'll never die.'[146] From then on, Angelo believes that these departed cinema spaces have 'souls', and that somewhere in London he'll find a place where all these souls, and the saturated emotion of decades of cinema-goers, all reside together: a place he fantasises as the 'Museum of Lost Cinema Spaces'.[147] He explains his concept of cinema spaces having 'souls' to a girl he meets in a movie memorabilia shop, saying: 'You can tear down the screen and bulldoze the walls, but you can never destroy the space itself.'[148]

Taking this alongside his belief that the disused cinemas have *souls* then, Angelo stands within the novel as voice for exactly the idea to which Royle introduces us in *The Matter of the Heart*:

namely, that these abandoned spaces *exceed* the 'produced', the 'actualized' and even the social, upon which de Certeau, Lefebvre and Quentin & Stevens rely so heavily in conceptualising urban space. Instead Angelo's idea that his cinema spaces live on after demolition (like the old St. George's hospital does after redevelopment), and that they survive somehow, even when no longer actualized through the human practices which they once housed, again shows the abandoned spaces of Royle's fiction working transhumanly, independently of human actualization. Like fields of affect, these spaces circulate, haunt and move characters to emotion, even after dereliction and demolition: that is, even when they are not physically manifest or actualized either in the landscape of the novel or in the consciousness of its characters.

The notion of affect proves even more useful in interrogating Angelo's engagement with abandoned cinemas: an obsession which plays a crucial role throughout *The Director's Cut*. In her posthumously published book, *The Transmission of Affect*, Teresa Brennan argues that if we are to agree that affects are capable of being transmitted from, say one person to another, or in Royle's case, between an emotionally-loaded space and individual characters, then we need to think of selfhood as something which is slightly more porous than we might like to believe. Brennan argues that the Western world demonstrates an obsession with keeping the body intact and impermeable, with the self being idealised as 'a private fortress, personal boundaries against the unsolicited emotional intrusions of the other'.[149] Yet, through their strong affective resonances and subsequent role in a 'two-way' dynamic in which the space's 'atmosphere [...] gets inside' the individual,[150] Royle's abandoned spaces act as an interface through which characters are given the opportunity to convene and merge with the others these spaces once housed, breaking down this idea of the impermeable self. For example, through gaining access to abandoned cinema spaces, Angelo 'felt the mingled emotions of a thousand departed cinema-goers', to the point that he 'now became one of them for a few brief seconds'.[151] Rather than appropriating or imposing his own agenda upon his beloved defunct cinemas, Angelo uses his access to the disused spaces as an opportunity to let the others that once resided within these spaces 'come through' and live again, albeit fleetingly. This proves that Angelo is capable of what Brennan describes as 'more permeable ways of being' than those which glorify the self as an emotionally contained discrete entity and thus deny the notion of affective transmission.[152] Through the character of Angelo therefore and his faith in cinema spaces' ability to 'live on' after their demolition or redevelopment, Royle suggests that abandoned spaces in particular possess an agency to either yield or withhold the transmission of affect.

Why Abandoned Spaces?

After a detailed examination of these two novels then, the issue remains as to why it might be abandoned buildings in particular that appeal to Royle as urban spaces which possess their own narrative agency beyond human actualization: an agency which is akin to that possessed by latent yet influential fields of affect. Why should Royle find the abandoned building to be particularly, as he expresses, 'teeming with ideas'?[153] To conclude, I would like to offer a few thoughts that might start to answer this question. Tim Edensor, who has written extensively on the aesthetics and cultural relevance of industrial ruins, argues that when industrial or institutional buildings are in operation, they work according to and as part of 'normative flows': networks of monetary exchange, production or 'commodity flows'.[154] Once abandoned however, Edensor notes that such spaces then become 'disembedded' from these flows, and open themselves up to assimilation into 'new human and non-human networks'.[155] Similarly, Rebecca Solnit describes how 'an urban ruin is a place that has fallen outside the economic life of the city', thus providing a home for practices which exist 'outside the ordinary production and consumption of the city'.[156] Abandoned buildings therefore offer Royle the ideal devices through which to explore the idea that urban space can work transhumanly, since they have ceased to be actualized through individual and collective human practice: the 'acts and gestures' which Lefebvre found so important to the production of space. The abandoned hospital and the disused cinema are no longer filled with the hectic day-to-day workings of the medical or leisure space, making it easier for Royle to thoroughly survey the potentialities and latencies which these buildings carry with them, and the agency that such spaces themselves (rather than the human subjects that usually busy the spaces with their action and noise) thus wield in subtly generating divergences in narrative action. In contemporary, late-capitalist Britain therefore, where large consumer 'chains' or corporations are guzzling up urban spaces (just like Angelo's beloved cinemas are forced to give way to bingo halls, theme pubs and 'soulless' multiplexes), abandoned and redeveloped sites are salient not merely because they stimulate a melancholic nostalgia for the past; instead, as Royle's fiction demonstrates, abandoned spaces and their redevelopment reveal how the re-shaping of our urban landscape is in danger not only of sanitising space, but also of controlling and restricting the fields and movements of affect which keep the city 'feeling' and alive.

Bibliography

Anderson, Ben. 'Becoming and being hopeful: towards a theory of affect' in *Environment and Planning D: Society and Space*. 24.5 (2006): 733-752.

Brennan, Teresa. *The Transmission of Affect*. New York: Cornell University Press, 2004.

Certeau, Michel de. *The Practice of Everyday Life*. Trans. Steven F. Randall. Berkeley; London: University of California Press,

1984.

Edensor, Tim. *Industrial Ruins*. Oxford: Berg, 2005.

Franck, Karen A., and Quentin Stevens (eds.). 'Tying Down Loose Space,' in *Loose Space: Possibility and Diversity in Urban Life*. Oxford: Routledge, 2005.

Lefebvre, Henri. *The Production of Space*. Trans. Donald Nicholson-Smith. Oxford: Blackwell, 1991.

— *Writings on Cities*. Trans. and ed. by Eleonore Kofman and Elizabeth Lebas. Cambridge, Massachusetts: Blackwell, 1996.

Lorimer, Hayden. 'Cultural geography: nonrepresentational conditions and concerns' in *Progress in Human Geography*, 32.4 (2008): 551-9.

Ninjalicious. *Access All Areas: A User's Guide to the Art of Urban Exploration*. Toronto: Infilpress, 2005.

Pile, Steve. 'Memory and the City', in *Temporalities: Autobiography and Everyday Life*. Ed. By Jan Campbell and Janet Harbord. Manchester: Manchester University Press, 2002: 111-27.

Royle, Nicholas. Interview with David Kendall. The Edge Magazine. 2007. http://www.theedge.abelgratis.co.uk/royleiview.htm

—- *The Matter of the Heart*. London: Abacus, 1997.

—- *The Director's Cut*. London: Abacus, 2000.

Solnit, Rebecca. *A Field Guide to Getting Lost*. New York; London: Penguin, 2006.

Postcards from the House of Light:
A Critical Introduction / A Creative Intervention

David Ashford

Postcard # 1

Five shuffle past a plate-glass door. Two men in coats and a family of three. A small girl topped with a knitted hat pulled along by her father and mother. Pass through a dark space of curving iron and into the light. A guard stoops to unlatch and seal the doors shut. In the next shot, a sheer glass-front onto something that might be a laboratory, or an observatory: a ceiling in motion, rapidly sweeping about to flood the white space and the reflective surface of the glass-screen with sun. The eye can make nothing of this. Nothing is substantial, nothing is still. Some futurist fantasy of a vast and abstract mechanism for the movement of shadow and light. Both building and a machine. But what? – the roof and the wall fully retract to reveal a colossal cage. Mok and Moina are kept here: the baby gorillas at London Zoo. Face pressed to the bars and chicken-wire one of the infants looks up to the right, the concrete-wall curling about to enclose him. In winter the House is shut – public in one half, the apes in the other. In summer the cage is revolved and the glass-screen pulled back – the infant gorillas occupying the complete circle, while the public watches from without.

In this motion picture by Lazlo Moholy-Nagy, the Gorilla House at London Zoo, by Berthold Lubetkin's firm Tecton, is hailed as the beginning of a new era, ushered in by the use of reinforced concrete.[157] And zoo-enclosures were a significant milestone for the modernist movement. For most of those working-class Londoners who flocked to see the gorilla-children in their new home, this was their first encounter with the new architecture. Built at a time when the works of the modernist mainstream, centred in Paris, remained for the most part on the drawing board, the Gorilla House, with subsequent enclosures by Tecton in London, Dudley and Whipsnade, was perceived to be providing a sane blueprint for the future development of the human metropolis. In fact, the project can be interpreted as a form of animal-testing. As science-historian Peder Anker has noted, Peter Chalmers-Mitchell, secretary of the Zoological Society, believed that if gorillas and penguins could be shown to thrive in 'the most unnatural conditions' the same would hold for the poor, who were in desperate need of being liberated from their "natural" conditions of criminal and filthy slums. 'It was thus of revolutionary importance to display thriving animals in an unnatural setting as if to prove that humans too could prosper in a new environment'.[158] Following wide-spread ruin in the course of the Blitz, this ambition would at last be realised, as the architect Lubetkin began to apply the modernist architecture he had pioneered at London Zoo to the problem of mass-housing. The kernel of that future city which we now inhabit is this Le Corbusian *machine for habitation* in London Zoo. This first House of Light.

The fate of the infant gorillas therefore holds peculiar horror. After six months in their new home Mok and Moina were dead; the bodies subjected to a Persian funeral, put in a cage on a roof in the sun, to be picked clean by carrion-crow.[159] The tussle over where to assign blame – to poor maintenance or to poor design, to careless owner or to thoughtless architect – must now seem a foreshadowing of the argument that would rage, in subsequent decades, over modernist mass-housing in the UK. In the course of this project I argue that these infant gorillas in their House of Light were not the victims of an oversight, as the architect maintained, but of a terrible mistake in the Cartesian philosophy underpinning modernist thought.

In addition to representing a turning-point in the history of modernism, the Gorilla House at London Zoo occupies an integral place in the crisis in Humanism identified by Jacques Derrida, considered at length in one of his last pieces, *The Animal That Therefore I Am* (2007). In this book, Derrida set out to track the systematic relegation of the Animal in philosophy back to the theoretical break initiated by Rene Descartes; the stark binary that defines the human by corralling every other species on the planet into a single concept, under a single name, The Animal. It is this consistent characterisation of the Animal as that which is deprived of the Logos, the right and power to respond, which is the root of the systematic misery inflicted on other animal species by humans, or on other humans unfortunate enough to have themselves been marked out as in some way "Animal". The Gorillas in the House of Light represent the culmination of this Enlightenment reduction of the Animal: the subjects are held in a fearsome geometry, a lyrical celebration of human reason. But this very extremity is also a symptom of societal unease – an example as striking as any cited by Derrida of an anthropocentric reinstitution of the superiority of the Human over the Animal that in fact testifies to the panic generated by 'humanity's second trauma'. Evolution: the knowledge that Man is intimately involved in everything that he had so long tried to disavow as other, as Animal.[160]

The fact that this House of Light was designed to hold *gorillas* is very significant. For this species possessed a peculiar cultural resonance in the early twentieth century. The full extent of the unease provoked by the creature is reflected in the otherwise inexplicable rise of the gorilla-related horror-film. One survey suggests that a hundred films with gorillas were produced between 1908 and 1948, and of these the vast majority were horror.[161] The titles of the first three films identified by this survey speak volumes about the particular anxieties this genre sought to play upon: *The Monkey Man, The Doctor's Experiment or Reversing Darwin's Theory,* and *Sherlock Holmes in the Great Murder*

Mystery. (The latter film particularly intriguing for the Edgar A. Poe style clash it seems to promise between the embodiment of the Enlightenment tradition himself and those primal forces that had come to be epitomised by Great Apes.) The gorilla had become the living embodiment of the emerging crisis of faith in Cartesian thought.

I embarked on a research project in order to explain why, relating insights gained in the course of my investigation to the perceived failure of the modernist intervention in British housing in the post-war period. But I soon found myself equally fascinated by other elements in this material that could find no outlet in the work of cultural criticism in which I was engaged. Most of the gorillas in the movies I viewed were played by men in gorilla costumes; a band of professional ape-impersonators, often taking passion for realism to alarming lengths. If no one has heard of Charlie Gemora, master of the art, in part this is because this remarkable actor would insist on having his name removed from the credits in order to maintain the realism of the production. On one occasion in the course of filming in a shipyard, Gemora was told by producers to remain in character throughout lunch, locked up in a cage on the side of the dock. In the half-hour that the film-crew were away, Gemora was savagely beaten with planks of wood by sailors, who were under the impression that they were tormenting a captive animal. Throughout this ordeal, Gemora did not break character.[162] What might such an actor have achieved with those supremely theatrical zoo-enclosures fashioned by Lubetkin? – consciously 'designing architectural settings for the animals in such a way as to present them dramatically to the public, in an atmosphere comparable to that of a circus'.[163]

Gemora would have instantly recognised the model or template for the Gorilla House in London. The 'intrinsic human ceremony' enacted by a porch that ushered the public into a darkened theatre. The sliding panel. The big reveal of a horror that figures the spectator's own primitive drives, held in a spotlight.[164] This was the Cabinet of Dr Caligieri. The freak-show of the Mad Scientist. In such films the ape might escape the cage, but the menace it poses to the boundary between Human and Animal is invariably swiftly eliminated. Lubetkin's theatre could not, for obvious reasons, permit such escapades! – but it nevertheless offered similar scope for a popular ritual of regression. The primitive drives that threatened civilised society were not permitted to fester in darkness but were rendered safe by being brought to light. The savagery in ourselves was made the subject of a system of knowledge and control; the atavist energies embodied by the gorilla were held in a containment-structure, a pattern based on Euclidean figures which testified to the all-encompassing power of the rational mind.

How might Charlie Gemora have re-activated the latent narrative-structure coded in this performance-space by the modernist architect? How might he have performed that tense interplay between systems of circulation and containment? How re-enacted the eternal gladiatorial sacrifice of the beast, now that the arena for this spectacle was operating on an unprecedented and overwhelming level of technological sophistication.

Now Gemora was dead any such performance could only take place in the mind. Like Wyndham Lewis's 'The Enemy of the Stars' – it would have to be 'Very Well Produced By You And Me'.[165] I began to toy with the idea of a fiction that would bring the King of the Gorilla-Men into conflict with that House of Light in Regent's Park, or rather, a series of such spaces, charting the modernist trajectory and interrogating the philosophy under-writing it. In so doing, I hoped to explore the interplay between physical and metaphorical. Neither is static and self-enclosed. But intersects with and impacts upon the other. In overlaying each site with my writing, through re-aligning each within a new continuum, I can radically reconfigure the semiotic codes of which each space is comprised. For the reader willing to participate in this fantasy, I can effect real transformation in the fabric of urban space.

Postcard # 2

Setting: – red sun on a 40-ft hill – the tidal-lake turned to blood – about a Black Mass; squatting toad and snake-headed bird, a complication of serpent-necked turtle, waiting for the Master, as the star sinks, into a supermodern imperial shopping-arcade of solid light.

This is the world's first prehistoric theme park, the original creation or resurrection of extinct animals – destined to roam as in their native state through the deep morass of Penge; a miniature Saurian bog. The still waters stubby with long snouts, trickling teeth, beneath lizard eyes empty and round, while Iguanodons (horny, lethargic and fat) face off a predator (grinning – reassembled all wrong! – a theropod turned to hell hound). Only the light moves. The island is enchanted. Potentates of the Wealden and Oolite, "fixed" for the instruction of the Great British Public; arranged, catalogued, a stillborn revival. Four iron columns, nine feet long, seven inches across, six-hundred bricks, thirty-eight casks of cement (ground from the fragments of a fine medieval hallway – a prescient exercise in Brutalism, this Gothic Revival!), with one-hundred feet of iron hoping, and twenty-feet of cube-inch-bar, constitute the bones, sinews and muscles of the largest. All to confirm mosaic record; to prove that God had a hand. The earliest reconstruction of the prehistoric world, organised by a proponent of what is now called "Intelligent Design", an expansion on that pioneering scientific-project conducted in Eden: *Fish-Lizard, Wing-lizard, Big-lizard, Last-lizard, Two-dog-tooth, Reptile-of-the-Wood*. . . .

The Animal is named;

And Man is the maker of worlds.

On this sunny evening, in the year nineteen-hundred-and-three,

Mrs. Kitty Calcutt, wife of the Retired Colonel, huddled over her stride, like a swift stork eyeing for eel, turned to meet the wooden bridge for Tertiary Island and leaned out over the parapet to watch the froth move on the water.

Not yet twenty-five, she felt haggard, outmoded; life no longer a spin of the wheel! For four years she had lived in a house set apart for the assistant to the British Consul to Siam; overlooking the river, she would wake to a skyline resplendent with stupa, orange-robed monks intoning prayers, see dancers in red silk move to heterophonic melodies on xylophone, oboe and drum by a sleepy gargantuan Buddha, a curving tube of bright gold. Only last year, she had travelled in the wake of the Eight-Nation Alliance, the international invasion to relieve the besieged legation district in Peking; had witnessed the Righteous Fists of Harmony, warrior-monks immune through faith to blade or bullet, reduced to a heap of fly-blown meat in the black reeking shell of the Yung Lo Ta Tien, the oldest and richest library in the world. She herself had helped "carve the melon", passing through the centre of the sprawling Meridian Gate into the Red Forbidden City and on to the Hall of Supreme Harmony; had ascended the three steps through a tettering of marble and jade to reach out and touch the woven tails of the three-leaved Dragon Throne.

And now she lived on her husband's army pension; her horizons had shrivelled. Eternal canyons of redbrick, fussily stuccoed and semidetatched, stockbroker-feudal London, smothered in brown fog distant but present, her world grown suddenly small, rage had tightened the skin round the skull, crushed up into deep grooves, fault-lined her face. She acknowledged with a sour twist of her lips the fractured and shuffled sedimentary-rock behind the fall. Some eminent prophet of science had manufactured this ersatz formation for the edification of the public mind. But, if those gentlemen had so easily faked the evidence for the process they hoped to prove, how could you trust anything they said? Kitty smiled, bitter. On the tree overhead, a magpie cackled.

Looked up saw something dark scrabble over the outcrop on Secondary Island. Frockcoat and stove-hat, white-whiskered, straightened and waved. Her heart thrashed the drum of her chest like a fish in a bag at a fairground. The grey suede glove, raised to the red light, gestured she cross the weir, a range of exposed rock, linking her own era to that of the ancient reptilian world; and shrank to a mound of black fabric, tipped with points of shiny black leather and gleaming beaver-skin, beneath the outstretched membranes of an irate pterodactyl. Man-shaped but foreign to this tableau. An occult force brooding a unholy spark in these inert golem like a sick inversion of the African fable of *How the Honey-Bee*: a Pourquois Story, to pass time while Kitty is deciding to risk herself to the weir.

Having been cast out of heaven and all, the devil was sulking a hot-head in hell, brooding over the beautiful universe that the Lord God Almighty made after casting him out. Now, Pandemonium was a fine piece of work in its way, an outstanding example of modern architecture. Sure, you had to shrink you to an imp if you wanted to get in, but for form and symmetry, for the dramatic interplay of light and shadow, it was perfect. Ah! – but what joy in the Ideal Home if surrounded by a stagnant circle of sometime friends with no scope to expand, to create, to nurture something organic, something living? – the devil was certainly stuck in a rut, and he resolved to start something new. If God could create an entire world in the space of seven days (Old Nick was a Biblical literalist), then why could not he, the Morning Star, the Supreme Commander of Thrones, Dominations, Princedoms, Virtues, Powers of the Northern Sky, not create just one animal, a small one perhaps, on a miniature-scale, but finely crafted. Why not? And so the tale goes the devil delved in the deep places of the underworld for precious minerals and stones, and mingled these with a scalding tear, to fashion the honey-bee from a clay of gold and jet. But for all that the devil could not breathe life into this intricate engine. So offered it up to the Lord for inspection. And the Lord God gasped at the beauty of the thing. And on the impact of the sacred breath the tiny creature stretched its crystal wings in the sun, and thenceforth sipped on liquid gold from the brightest and most beautiful things in creation.

Kitty jolted forward; decided. If he was going to play the fool. Banged to the end of the bridge. Slithered down a bank into a herd of tapir. And placed her heavy booted foot with care on the first slick stone. Then goated from rock to rock. Her music-hall full-blood back in a flash. The Sensational Kitty Barlow! The One and Only, lithe and trippy girl's girl of Gatti's-in-the-Road. The good old days like a short stiff gin stung her heart into happiness. She was back at the beginning for a fresh start. She dodged the outstretched maw of some massive half-submerged marine reptile, and skittered up the bank through a tangle of fern and gingko to a plateau of rock at the top, under a crag capped with poised pterodactyl. . . . Steadied herself and panted prettily, fixing her eye on the sable aristocratic outfit; 'Hello!'

'Hello to you.'

'What are you writing?'

The moleskine snapped to. 'I'm not writing.'

Kitty swung her lacy parasol at a tuft of coarse grass: 'What are you reading?'

'Nothing. My to-do-list!'

The skin about the thin mouth tightened to a dry, cold grin:

'I'm leaving tomorrow. Barnum's circus is off to Chicago. I've decided to go with the gorilla!'

In frame small, but intensely powerful, fairly handsome, with a sort of weird Eastern grace, despite certain slight oddities of proportion, Sir Alfred Jermyn had never seemed to look quite right, both face and figure were somehow subtly repellent. Learning was in his blood, for his grandfather, Sir Robert, had been an anthropologist of note, while his great-great-grandfather Sir Wade Jermyn, was one of the earliest explorers of the Congo, author of a peculiar monograph asserting that the region held by the Onga and Kaliri concealed colossal crumbling ruins of a prehistoric white civilisation. But Sir Alfred Jermyn was no scholar; his tastes reflected the unsettling physical features that characterised that unfortunate bloodline. At twenty he had joined a band of music-hall performers, playing a caricatured swell, womanising, drinking and gambling; perhaps the one such impersonator in the history of vaudeville to hail from a genuinely aristocratic background; his signature-song *The Black Sheep of the Family*. Sir Alfred Jermyn presented a doubled face to his unknowing audience. The real deal masquerading as itself. At thirty he'd married Kitty's professional partner and best-friend, the drag-king Linda Slow, famous for playing a dissolute toff, not entirely unlike himself; and at thirty-six he had deserted wife and child to travel with an itinerant American circus as handler of a huge bull gorilla, of lighter colour than average, and the source of a singular fascination for Sir Alfred. Who was in short something straight out of H. P. Lovecraft.

Now, slowly rising to stand; slim and stylishly cut, close and tall.

Kitty's eyes swivelled down quick to meet the pattern of the silk waist-coat. 'You are taking a great risk with that monster!' she muttered. 'You don't know what you're doing!'

'On the contrary,' suede smoothing her tight hazel:

'I know that beast. I know that beast. I know that beast like the back of my hand.'

Playful, poking the shirt with a pert forefinger: 'But that Thing will murder you!'

Laughed; 'I assure you that's quite impossible.'

'Oh *really* Professor!' waggling her head.

Stooping to breathe in the cool and curious scent of her forehead: 'We don't hang lions for murder. We'd never put a dog on trial. And that's because murder is an act of will. You see, Mrs. Kitty Calcutt, in this, our enlightened age, only a rational mind can be guilty of murder. It's a sign, I say, of that divine faculty, for conscious thought, that sets our Human Race apart from the merely Animal. . . .'

'Okay Mister – not murder but kill!'

'Only careless men are killed by machines: – Now the wisest heads in Europe will say that that beautiful bull gorilla is a sort of organic machine; fellow's programmed to act, but there's no more thought or spirit there than there is in the tune of a pianola.'

'I don't think you believe a word you're saying!'

Smiling faint in the deep dusk; 'No.'

'Aren't you afraid?

'Aren't *you* afraid?

'Why me afraid? I'm not about to go off like some crazy man and box a gorilla!'

'And yet you are here – in a swamp at night – surrounded by monsters!'

With mock-motherly concern: 'They're not real, you know!'

A grey glove slapped the rump of a guana: 'It's real alright.'

'But it's made of stone – it's artificial!

'But my gorilla is no less *manufactured*; he is you might say in an *unreal position*.'

Kitty had seen the two rehearsing an exceedingly clever boxing-match in a tent on Peckham Rye the previous Saturday. Having steeled herself to approach the beast, Kitty had renewed her former acquaintance with Sir Alfred Jermyn, broken in a green rage when she had been told that Linda Slow no longer thought it quite proper for her, now married, to be tipping the velvet.

Kitty had only imagined the scene in the Actors Church; the same two grooms at the altar. They'd married exactly that which they'd seen of themselves in the other: a double-backed *Comedy Lion*. News of their wrecked marriage piqued Kitty's interest. In any event she had at last consented to meet the image of her ex-g.f. in the parkland beneath Crystal Palace.

To encounter this freakish and grim set-piece! this monster-infected spoof of a Summer Romance! Hadn't she once done a skit just like this moment with Linda? Some ghoul haunted backdrop, busy with big bats, the stage-floor messy with python? Kitty raised face to meet the mask of the clown above her with new understanding, replaying that once familiar comic-routine.

Miss Kitty. You are absurd; – where's the romance in a Bat!

Lord Slow. Why the bat is the most romantic thing in the world! Have you not seen him, hung tall and dark, scaling an ivied wall, or flitting to keep faith at some midnight tryst?

Miss Kitty. With a cow in the field!

Lord Slow. With a bride in the bed! It's true he's not particular but nor was Casanova!

Miss Kitty. He's a love rat!

Lord Slow. Even rats can play Cupid.

Miss Kitty. [*Aside:*] He's so ironic – so Byronic!

Lord Slow. [*Embracing Miss Kitty:*] My dear believe me when I say that I am that rat! [*Putting a pistol to his head:*] If you can't have me – no one will!

Miss Kitty. [*Distraught:*] I really don't know! So few men have a capacity to feel!

Lord Slow. [*Kneading her breast:*] So few men have the opportunity!

Miss Kitty. [*Swoons into his arms; then raises her head to address the punters.*]

I'm a timid flow'r of innocence
Papa says I have no sense!
Not too strict but rather free
Yet as right as right can be!
Never forward, never bold
Not too hot – and not too cold!

When a nice young man is nigh
I'll faint away with tearful cry!
But won't come to while thus embraced
Till of my pouting lips he taste!

Kitty – raising her pinks on cue, in expectant pout – was kissed by the lecherous Lord. Spluttered, pushed away; Kitty had come tonight intent on cuckolding her militant spouse but now it came to the crunch – wasn't sure she wanted the risk. Pity this girl. Bound to some decrep. The Colonel hadn't stood to attention since receiving that medal for surviving the Siege of Khartoum. She'd not married the man, but a lifetime ticket with a first-rate travel-agency called the Empire. That was understood. Her boring husband had broken faith first. Lord Slow, or was it Sir Alfred, *should* be encouraged to ferret her S-bend loose. That backbreaking corset represented her state of suburban oppression – and should peel instanter! She shuffled her velvet travelling-jacket over her shoulders and picked at the snowflake-embossed buttons on the waist-coat in front. Fingers moving through fabric, flickering over each new plane of cloth, pushed into the cleft of her high ruffled collar, snapped free the taut band bracing his trousers, forcing an entry every which way; the antennae of two loving insects in slow-mo.

Kitty's chignon wobbled; suede rasped the skin of her neck.
'Not here.'
'Why not?'
'Because we've got us peeping-Toms!'
Two ragamuffin boys on the neighbouring island were waiting for the culmination to this vaudevillian freebie with evident relish, squinting intent as the two actors faded fast into the murk of their south London swamp. Lord Slow hurled a handful of gold pieces over the water, together with a series of ear-withering obscenities, carrot and stick: the latter measure proving rather too effective – the scamps running off not

stopping to pick up the coin. Lord Slow shrugged, and pushed Kitty into the thicket behind the pterodactyl. Staggered half-dressed, toppled giggling to the ground beneath the smiling snout of a lizard, not unlike that of an Anglican priest, smug and amused, benignly indulgent, witnessing the antics of that naughty mammal. Lord Slow cracked open the swan-bill corset a white shell flung off into the night and stooped to dab at Kitty's splay tits, laid out 2 fried eggs on a porcelain plate. Her grey eyes hungered from her pale wasted face to meet the Nordic mask drawn level hard and cold as an ice-sheet. Kitty stretched her hand to the slackened waistband and murmured ingénue sing-song her signature hit:

I've got a little cat
And I'm very fond of that
But I'd rather have a bow-wow
Wow. Wow. Wow. Wow.

Kitty had revived, had coaxed, with slender beckoning finger, back into the light, some terrible lizard of the ancient world; some sauropod, stretching out, slow-witted, on its stout cord of a throat, to sway on high a blunt silly head, urgent, uncompli-cated, single-minded, unutterably stupid. Life forms moving on a different clock, cunning from before When Dinosaurs Ruled. Till at length Bronto spat and retched, stammered out name and slobbered, a sleepy mephitic reptile, slithering, shrivelling, back into that dark place from whence it came. . . .

Lord Slow ran a thick red mark through Item No.3 in his notebook; and, having made this final effort, let fall his blank mask to dream in the dirt.

Kitty yawned contented, and traced the shape of a serpent up in the stars overhead. Perhaps she *might* run away to the US. Gathered wool. Tried to remember *something* concerning Chicago. Weren't there gangsters there? Wasn't a railway up in the sky? something to do with a scandal? Or maybe a man as strange as Lord Slow (or was it Sir Alfred) but money-grubbing and badly-dressed. She might come to like the United States. But so much depended. Her eyes came to rest on the two Iguanodon, huge and silver, sculpted in moonlight. Nothing ever ended but must return, a lonely ghost. But who will raise you up . . . when you've lost your bedstead, And you can't find your way home. . .

Kitty fell away from the blades of starlight moving over paradise and into the land.

Her name etched in acid, a sequence of letters as yet unknown to science, halved, fastened up like a zipper – with another story written in an alien genre; now combined to forge something new.

So began the career of Edgar Calcutt, a monster in the House of Light.

Bibliography

John Allan, *Lubetkin: Architecture and the Tradition of Progress*, RIBA Publications, 1992

Jacques Derrida, *The Animal That Therefore I Am*, trans. David Wills, Fordham University Press, 2007.

Louise Kehoe, *In This Dark House: A Memoir*, Viking, 1996

John Allan, Morley van Sternberg, *Berthold Lubetkin*, Merrell Publishers, 2002

Wyndham Lewis, "Enemy of the Stars", *Collected Poems and Plays*, ed. Alan Munton, Carcanet: Manchester, 1979.

Di Brandt: A Mennonite Girl
in the Heart of the City

Jenna Butler

Brandon, Manitoba-based poet Di Brandt possesses a deep connection to the landscape in which she grew up; a connection that is one of both affirmation and ambivalence. Brandt was raised in the small Mennonite settlement of Reinland, Manitoba[166] and left in her mid-teens to attend college in Winnipeg. She began to write after settling in an urban community vastly different from the open expanses of the prairies of her childhood. Her first book of poetry, *questions i asked my mother*, was published in 1987 and established Brandt as a writer to watch, while simultaneously starting her on the lengthy path of dislocation from her Mennonite roots. Over the next several decades, Brandt would continue to write and publish, and through the exploration of her Mennonite past, simultaneously gain an avid non-Mennonite readership and alienate herself completely from the community of her childhood.

In more recent years, Brandt's work has moved from an exploration and interrogation of the paternal nature of Mennonite society to a focus on ecopoetics and feminist ways to find 'home' in the natural world.

Brandt was the first member of her family in 400 years to abandon the Mennonite lifestyle and move to an urban centre. Although her break with her community to live in the city and write was supported by a more ethnically-aware government during the '60s and '70s, this same need to write, to explore her Mennonite roots, caused an irreparable rift between Brandt and her family.

Brandt's writing goes beyond a simple homage to the prairie

landscape and into something much more fraught. Yes, she is fascinated by the landscape in which she grew up, and specifically the place of her people in that landscape, but her relationship to the land remains that of an immigrant. She writes as a newcomer to a space that is a historical battleground, where existing stories have been overwritten by those who have only just arrived. In spite of the Mennonite celebration of the land, Brandt claims that '[i]t is impossible for [her] to write the land. This land that [she] love[s], this wide, wide prairie, this horizon, this sky, this great blue overhead, big enough to contain every dream, every longing',[167] possesses a number of undercurrents for her people to which Brandt is ambivalent. She is wary of her culture's disempowerment of the First Nations people in the name of agricultural progress; she recognizes that in a bid to make a home for themselves on the Canadian Prairies, the Mennonites helped the Canadian government to take from the First Nations people their traditional nomadic way of life.

It is this uneasy understanding of her province's—indeed, her country's—dark history that proves one of the impetuses for Brandt's award-winning collection *Now You Care*. For several years, Brandt was resident in Windsor, located in the infamous Windsor-Detroit industrial corridor in southern Ontario. Here, surrounded not by the vast spaces of her childhood, but by the ravages of industrial excess, she '[understood] [her] heritage in a whole other way. The Mennonites had a great sense of responsibility to the land, of living close to the rhythm of the seasons and trying to live simply and plainly on the land so [one] [could] have an intimate relationship with it'.[168] This sense of bewilderment and despair at the factory-obsessed culture of southern Ontario is visible at once in the opening poem of the collection, a serial elegy to the land as it was before the rush of industry:

Zone: <le Détroit>

after Stan Douglas

1
Breathing yellow air
here, at the heart of the dream
of the new world,
the bones of old horses and dead Indians
and lush virgin land, dripping with fruit
and the promise of wheat,
overlaid with glass and steel
and the dream of speed:
all these our bodies
crushed to appease
the 400 & I gods
of the Superhighway,
NAFTA, we worship you,
hallowed be your name,
here, where we are scattered
like dust or rain in ditches,
the ghosts of passenger pigeons
clouding the silver towered sky,
the future clogged in the arteries
of the potholed city,
Tecumseh, come back to us
from your green grave,
sing us your song of bravery
on the lit bridge over the black river,
splayed with grief over the loss
of its ancient rainbow coloured
fish swollen joy.
Who shall be fisher king
over this poisoned country,
whose borders have become

a mockery,
blowing the world to bits
with cars and trucks and electricity and cars,
who will cover our splintered
bones with earth and blood,
who will sing us back into -[169]

Paying homage to Canadian artist Stan Douglas and crying out to T.S. Eliot, 'Zone: <le Détroit>' plays upon the same notion of the failed utopia of modernism that underwrote so many of Douglas's installations. Brandt's deep despair at the industrial behemoth of Windsor-Detroit is evident from the outset in her bitter observation that we are '[b]reathing yellow air/here, at the heart of the dream/of the new world' (1-3), the new world that her people, among others, sought so long to find. A formerly agrarian dream of simplicity and plenty in this 'lush virgin land, dripping with fruit/and the promise of wheat' (5-6) has been overwritten by a contemporary industrial dream of more and more, as fast as we can get it. The simple ways of life that her culture holds dear have been sidelined, 'crushed to appease/the 400 & I gods/of the Superhighway' (11-12); the past has been paved over and 'the future [is] clogged in the arteries/of the potholed city' (19-20). For a former Mennonite girl from Reinland, this abuse of the natural world and the all-pervading capitalist culture is something completely alien:

> Once upon a time, I lived in a tiny Mennonite farming village in south-central Manitoba, called Reinland, the 'clean land'. ... My village was located in the very heart of the Mennonite world, in the middle of southern Manitoba, in the middle of the North American continent, in the middle of the world, as we thought.
>
> We told an elaborate but fixed story about ourselves as Mennonites in Reinland ... The rest of the world, for us, was

other, but as I found out when I got there, it was not at all other in the way we had imagined, in the way we'd been told. Its otherness, I could see immediately, was not the otherness of people lounging indifferently on the road to hell, but consisted rather in [sic] a completely different set of terms, a different set of rules to live by, and I wanted very much to know what they were.[170]

In Windsor, Brandt discovers some of the rules these 'others' live by. At the same time that she casts back to her Mennonite roots, trying to make sense of Windsor's vast industrial alienation from the landscape in which she grew up, from the true landscape underlying the city itself, she also finds herself reaching out to 'others' to stop the predations of heavy industry. In this case, the 'others' are the ones who came before, the First Nations people for whom the land was sacred. *'Tecumseh, come back to us/from your green grave'* (21-22), she pleads, wondering who is expected to heal and rule this shattered landscape. Who is to offer balm? When the voices of those who have gone before are silent, who is left to 'cover our splintered/bones with earth and blood' (34-35) and, through music, sing us back into being?

What kind of half-life, Brandt seems to say, are we living in such closed-in industrial areas? When all is devoted to keeping the machine of heavy industry in constant movement, what are we as individuals but parts for that machine? This visceral sense of disconnection and fear is immediately visible in the second poem of the series, where Brandt very literally breaks humans down into nothing more than parts; in this case, for organ donation:

2
See how there's no one going to Windsor,
only everyone coming from?
Maybe they've been evacuated,

maybe there's nuclear war,
maybe when we get there we'll be the only ones.
See all those trucks coming toward us,
why else would there be rush hour on the 401
on a Thursday at nine o'clock in the evening?
I counted 200 trucks and 300 cars
and that's just since London.
See that strange light in the sky over Detroit,
see how dark it is over Windsor?
You know how people keep disappearing,
you know all those babies born with deformities,
you know how organ thieves follow tourists
on the highway and grab them at night
on the motel turnoffs,
you know they're staging those big highway accidents
to increase the number of organ donors?
My brother knew one of the guys paid to do it,
$100,000 for twenty bodies
but only if the livers are good.
See that car that's been following us for the last hour,
see the pink glow of its headlights in the mirror?
That's how you know.
Maybe we should turn around,
maybe we should duck so they can't see us,
maybe it's too late,
maybe we're already dead,
maybe the war is over,
maybe we're the only ones alive.[171]

Why are all the cars coming *from* Windsor, she wonders? Is it
really nuclear war? No; instead, it is the routine mass exodus of
workers leaving industrial Windsor behind for their homes in the
suburbs and surrounding countryside. Detroit, that massive,
round-the-clock complex of factories and warehouses, is still

visible as 'that strange light in the sky' (11), whereas the dark has settled over Windsor as the workers depart for home. Yet the chain of departing vehicles evokes a horror-story response in Brandt; who are the people fleeing from? From there, it is a short leap to other aspects of life in a major urban centre that are the stuff of nightmares: people disappearing, the birth of deformed babies, the presence of organ thieves. Ultimately, the only other sign of company on the road (other than the stream of departing traffic), the car behind Brandt, is seen as a potential threat. In the midst of so much noise, traffic and industry, everything that makes a community has been stripped away. '[M]aybe we're the only ones alive' (31), Brandt muses. The reader is left to wonder, in such an environment of dislocation and fear, what kind of life could that be?

What kind of life, indeed, where the city itself is killing its inhabitants? In the third poem in the series, Brandt searches for the wild and the untainted in the heart of the urban sprawl. What she finds is something completely other, dark and disturbing; the amputated flesh of those infected by the city's myriad of ailments.

3
So there I am, sniffing around
the railroad tracks
in my usual quest for a bit of wildness,
weeds, something untinkered with,
goldenrod, purple aster, burdocks,
defiant against creosote,
my prairie blood surging
in recognition and fellow feeling,
and O god, missing my dog,
and hey, what do you know,
there's treasure here
among these forgotten weeds,

so this is where they hang out,
all those women's breasts
cut off to keep our lawns green
and dandelion free,
here they are, dancing
their breastly ghost dance,
stirring up a slight wind in fact
and behaving for all the world
like dandelions in seed,
their featherwinged purple nipples
oozing sticky milk,
so what am I supposed to do,
pretend I haven't seen them
or like I don't care
about all these missing breasts,
how they just vanish
from our aching chests
and no one says a word,
and we just strap on fake ones
and the dandelions keep dying,
and the grass on our lawns
gets greener and greener
and greener [172]

Searching for a hint of the land she knows is there *somewhere*, buried beneath the concrete and rebar of Windsor's urban core, Brandt experiences a disconcerting encounter with the true face of what many have considered a North American Eden:

America's oldest and most cherished fantasy ... is that of the land as a "maternal 'garden,'" a place of bountiful abundance, nurturance, and nonalienation (171-72). The promise of the 'New World' was the promise of a return to Eden, a homecoming: a 'regression from the cares of adult life and a return to the primal warmth of womb or breast in a feminine landscape' (173).[173]

Here, while Brandt hunts for 'a bit of wildness,/weeds, something untinkered with' (3-4), she very literally returns to the maternal breast in the disturbing discovery of 'all those women's breasts/cut off to keep our lawns green/and dandelion free' (14-16). This essential loss of the feminine, the very ability to nurture life, has been caused by nothing so mundane as our need to douse our lawns in pesticides and chemicals to keep them an unblemished green. In return for our deliberate flouting of the unspoiled land, the 'New World' we so greedily claimed, Brandt seems to say, we have robbed ourselves of all that nourishes us. Woman represents all that is sheltering, a concrete sense of home. By losing the ability to nourish her children, she, like the corrupted natural world around her, is no longer a safe place to linger.

Brandt's focus on our transformation of the New World Eden into a modern-day wasteland, failing to learn from our mistakes or the lessons of those Indigenous peoples whose lengthy histories precede us, is one I find resonating in much of my own work. While conducting my PhD research into Brandt's poetics, I began writing a series of long poems entitled *Memory in the Blood*, a phrase borrowed from First Nations writer Paula Gunn Allen[174]. Allen uses this phrase to allude to the passing on of a common cultural memory from one generation to the next amongst the First Nations peoples of North America. In my poetry, I have adapted this phrase to the settler culture in the New World; learning, or failing to learn, through its mistakes, through its refusal, in many cases, to heed the traditional histories and teaching stories of those cultures who came before, and very often, paying the price in blood. The series looks at several little-known historical Canadian disasters, including the Halifax Explosion, the Hillcrest Mine disaster, and the Frank Slide. All of the poems in the collection examine the treacherous interface between the New World and the incoming settler cultures.

One such poem in the series is entitled 'Frank Slide, 1903'. The town of Frank was built at the foot of Turtle Mountain, Alberta in the early 1900s. The founders of the town refused to heed the warnings of the local First Nations bands that the mountain was geologically unstable; indeed, their name for it was The Mountain That Moves. Incoming settlers built homes in the town and found work in the mines, swelling Frank's population to 600 souls. The mining town continued in innocent prosperity as the underground tremors worsened. In the days leading up to the Frank Slide, the shafts of Turtle Mountain were considered 'self-mining', as tremors loosened coal and rock alike from the tunnel walls and the workers had to do nothing but fill the cars and send them up to the surface. The mountain's warnings continued unheeded until the early morning of April 29, 1903, when Turtle Mountain moved again. Nearly 90 million tonnes of limestone sheared away from its face and buried the sleeping town of Frank completely.

One of the worst disasters in Canadian history, the Frank Slide speaks volumes to me of those concepts Brandt explores in *Now You Care*: the notion of our growing displacement, in this 'New Eden', from the landscape in which we live, and the history and knowledge of those cultures that have come before us. In an age of unchecked growth across North America, the question begs answering: what, if anything, have we learned from the past? Will we move forward with a sense of memory in the blood, or will we, like the settlers in Frank, continue doggedly along the path of our own mistakes?

Frank Slide, 1903
I.
its cree name is
the mountain that moves

this town has grown

by accretion layers coalescing
outward from epicenter

on main street
the bar opens at five
when the miners get off work
closes just past one
long enough for
the nightshift men
to drop some coin

above the tack shop
the milliner shears
bolts of velvet damask
brocade packed by mule train
over the pass from calgary
blinding herself slowly
by candlelight embroidery
incongruous luxury next to
gingham oilcloth

down creekside
the boarding house
churns with travelers
crowsnest tradesmen hacks with
satchels carpet bags
leaking fragrant tinctures

above the town mineshafts
riddle hillsides
dawn and dusk a thread of men
bisects the grade

the children here

are born to fire the lantern light of it
know only the coming and going of
fathers in darkness

II.
tremors shake coal
loose from ceilings shafts
nightshift loads up the cars
veterans alone
frown at the sway
of track and buttress
wary of hills that
surrender up their veins

the pulse comes
like breath rock spinning
predatory through jackpine
clapboard leaning its weight
onto the rumpled cockles of
mine town

local drunk
swings out of the bar
jigs his trousers down
in the street
accordioned to his knees
by aftershock glares
into gloom with
bleary eyes

calls it too much drink and
shambles off home

III.
level two
already underwater
in darkness the river
inches up passageways
gathers men silently with
subterranean fingers
afterdamp claims
what water cannot reach

remains of nightshift find
a likely seam find
picks scattered amongst boulders
begin the laborious climb
through a hundred feet of rockfall
of bodies

grind of their working
the only barrier between
themselves and the dark the sound
of water pooling

IV.
dawn the town
extricates itself counting absences
like amputations
construction camp livery stables
homes creviced under rock
spokane flyer halted silent
on dead end tracks

the miners break surface
at first light perch where
the lamphouse stood

stare down the revised face
of their mountain

the dead are assumed not counted

there are those
dragged from remnants of
houses edging town
still alive but
transfigured somehow
about the eyes
by that silent rush by
the sound of falling

V.
the mine is unearthed
one month later
tunnels dank with rot
 among the workers
 those who escaped
level one surviving pit pony
chews timber drinks seepage
blinks at the ring of
sudden headlamps
incredulous men

level two underwater
no survivors
just that horse

VI.
they mend the tracks first
each day the flyer brings
more men workers from the states

who will rebuild
without knowing the story

they site the town
where it has always been
at the ragged eastern foot
of the mountain that devoured it
build clapboard houses
that hug the slopes blaze
roads around the smaller boulders

on the hill
the mine chokes beneath
underbrush small tremors
clack the shafts
like bones like dice

pit pony done to death
by too many oats on
timber ragged stomach
by brandy

VII.
the roots of the mountain
move in high wind
town at its buckled knees
backlit by the imminence of
its own demise

up the valley
punched tin lamps dot the hillside
days clocked by iron clangor
picks and carts
new tracks overwriting history

this the way of all
frontier settlements

rebuild
sing over the bones

tend the children

Bibliography

Bailey Nurse, Donna, 'Di Brandt: Poems of passionate accusation'
, *Quill & Quire,* 70:6, 1

Brandt, Di, *Now You Care* (Toronto: Coach House Books, 2003)

Brandt, Di, *So this is the world & here I am in it* (Edmonton: NeWest
Press, 2007)

Brandt, Di, qtd. in Jeff Gundy's 'New Maps of the Territories: On
Mennonite Writing' , *The Georgia Review* LVII/4 (2003), 877

Kolodny, Annette, qtd. in Cheryl Lousley's 'Home on the Prairie?
A Feminist and Postcolonial Reading of Sharon Butala, Di
Brandt, and Joy Kogawa' , *Interdisciplinary Studies in Literature
and Environment* 8.2 (2001), 71

Suggested Additional Reading

Brandt, Di, *Agnes in the sky* (Winnipeg, Turnstone Press, 1990)

Brandt, Di, *Jerusalem, beloved* (Winnipeg: Turnstone Press, 1995)

Brandt, Di, *mother, not mother* (Toronto: Mercury Press, 1992)

Brandt, Di, *questions i asked my mother* (Winnipeg, Turnstone Press, 1987)

Brandt, Di, *Speaking of Power: The Poetry of Di Brandt*, ed. by Tanis MacDonald (Waterloo, Ontario: Wilfrid Laurier University Press Poetry Series, 2006)

Brandt, Di, *Wild Mother Dancing: Maternal Narrative in Canadian Literature* (Winnipeg: University of Manitoba Press, 1993)

Endnotes

1   Kalle Lasn, *Culture Jam: How to Reverse America's Suicidal Customer Binge – and Why We Must* (London: HarperCollins, 2000, p.19)

2   Naomi Klein, *No Logo* (London: Flamingo, 2001, p.287)

3   Kalle Lasn, *Culture Jam* (London: HarperCollins, 2000, p.131)

4   Ibid (p.164)

5   Marshall McLuhan, *Culture is Our Business*, (New York: Ballantine Books, 1970, p.66)

6   Kalle Lasn, *Culture Jam* (London: HarperCollins, 2000, p.123)

7   Jack Napier, www.billboardliberation.org

8   Naomi Klein, *No Logo* (London: Flamingo, 2001, p.291)

9   Erik Triantafillou, 'All the Instruments Agree', in *Paper Politics* by Josh McPhee (Oakland, California: PM Press, 2010, p.23)

10 www.bbc.co.uk, 'Paint daubed across Banksy mural', 06/04/2009.

11 see Dylan Mathews, *War Prevention Works: 50 Stories of People Resolving Conflict*, (London: Oxford Research Group, 2001, p.16-17)

12 www.nytimes.com, 'Artists Embellish Walls With Political Visions', 11/04/2010

13 Jeff Ferrell, *Tearing Down the Streets: Adventures in Urban Anarchy*, (London: Palgrave MacMillan, 2001, p.205)

14 Naomi Klein, *No Logo* (London: Flamingo, 2001, p.285)

15 Sam Sebren quoted in *Paper Politics* by Josh McPhee (Oakland, California: PM Press, 2010, p.45)

16 Claude Moller quoted in Ibid (p.51)

17 Dylan Miner, 'Existence', in Ibid (p.131)

18 Erik Triantafillou, 'All the Instruments Agree', in Ibid (p.24)

19 Emily Pohl-Weary, 'Notes on Postering Public Space: Can DIY Pirates Reclaim Your Downtown?', www.hackcanada

.com

20 Ibid.

21 These issues are addressed in publications such as: *Symbols in Northern Ireland*, Anthony Buckley (ed), (Belfast: The Institute of Irish Studies, 1998); Neil Jarman, 'Troubled images: the iconography of loyalism' *Critique of Anthropology 12*, (1992) pp.133-45; Bill Rolston, *Drawing support: murals in the North of Ireland* (Belfast: Beyond the Pale Publications, 1992); Bill Rolston, *Drawing support 2: murals of war and peace*, (Belfast: Beyond the Pale Publications, 1995).

22 Neil Jarman, 'Painting landscapes: the place of murals in the symbolic construction of urban space' in *Symbols in Northern Ireland*, Anthony Buckley (ed), (Belfast: The Institute of Irish Studies, 1998).

23 Tim Pat Coogan, *The Troubles: Ireland's Ordeal 1966-1996 and the Search for Peace*, (London: Arrow Books, 1996) p.472.

24 The list of murals in Northern Ireland from Conflict Archive on the Internet at the University of Ulster, many of them with accompanying images, has been compiled by Dr. Jonathan McCormick, and can be found at http://cain.ulst.ac.uk/mccormick/index.html

25 *Come Dine with Me- Belfast: Series 3, Episode 9*, Granada Productions for Channel 4, first broadcast on 3rd August 2006.

26 Robert McLiam Wilson, *Eureka Street*, (London: Vintage Books, 1998), p212.

27 Robin Morgan, *The Demon Lover: On the Sexuality of terrorism*, (London: Mandarin, 1990), p77.

28 Neil Jarman, 'Painting landscapes: the place of murals in the symbolic construction of urban space' in *Symbols in Northern Ireland*, Anthony Buckley (ed), (Belfast: The Institute of Irish Studies, 1998).

29 Seamus Heaney, *Opened Ground: Poems 1966-1996*, (London:

Faber and Faber, 1998), p458

30 Examples of the work of the Bogside Artists and their mission statement can be found at http://www.bog sideartists.com/

31 Allen Feldman, *Formations of Violence: The Narrative of the Body and Political Terror in Northern Ireland*, (Chicago and London: The University of Chicago Press, 1991), pp.28-41

32 The Battle of the Bogside was a communal riot in the Nationalist Bogside area of Derry from 12th-14th August 1969 that subsequently spread throughout the city and province. It is seen as being one of the antecedents, or possibly even one of the first riots of, the Troubles. Details can be found in: *Northern Ireland: A Chronology of the Troubles 1968-1993*, Paul Bew and Gordon Gillespie (eds), (Dublin: Gill & Macmillan Ltd, 1993), p17

33 Thus in Freud's essay 'The Uncanny' he suggests that 'if someone dreams of a certain place or a certain landscape and, while dreaming, thinks to himself, "I know this place, I've been here before," this place can be interpreted as repre-senting his mother's [...] womb."' Freud also suggests that the uncanny or *unheimlich,* that is, the unhomely, is what was once familiar or homely, but is no longer. Sigmund Freud, 'The Uncanny' in *The Uncanny* Translated by David McLintock, with an introduction by Hugh Haughton (London: Penguin Books, 2009), P.151. Subsequent refer-ences are to this edition.

34 The term *chora* is often translated as womb or receptacle, but 'Kristeva seems to something in mind that belongs to each person in particular before he or she develops clear borders of his or her own personal identity. In this early psychic space, the infant experiences a wealth of drives [...] that could be extremely disorientating and destructive were it not for the infant's relation with his or her mother's body. Her phrase "the semiotic *chora*" reminds the reader that the

chora is the space in which the meaning that is produced is semiotic: the [...] rhythms, and intonations of an infant who does not yet know how to use language to refer to objects.' See Noelle McAfee, *Julia Kristeva* (Routledge: New York and London, 2004), p.19

35   In his essay 'The Uncanny,' Freud argues that 'The study of dreams, fantasies and myths has taught us that anxiety about one's eyes, the fear of going blind, is quite often a substitute for the fear of castration.' Freud, 'The Uncanny' p.139

36   Robert Musil, *The Man Without Qualities* in n *Vienna A Traveller's Literary Companion* edited by Donald G.Daviau (Berkeley: California: Whereabouts Press, 2008), pp.154-5. Subsequent references are to this edition.

37   Ibid., p.153.

38   Lilian Fachinger, 'Vienna Passion' in *Vienna Passion* in *Vienna A Traveller's Literary Companion,* p.229.

39   Rainer Maria Rilke, The First Elegy of the Duino Elegies in *The Selected Poetry of Rainer Maria Rilke,* edited and trans-lated by Stephen Mitchell with an introduction by Robert Hass (Picador: London, 1987), p.151.

40   Rubén, Dario, *The Selected Poems* translated by Lysander Kemp, University of Texas, Austin, 1988 (http://www.dariana.com/R_Dario_poems.html#nocturne3), [accessed 9 February 2010]

41   T.S. Eliot, 'Little Gidding' No.4 of 'Four Quartets' (http://www.tristan.icom43.net/quartets/gidding.html   ) [accessed 24 April 2006]

42   Henri Lefebvre, *The Production of Space,* trans. Donald Nicholson-Smith, (Oxford: Blackwell Publishing, 1991). p. 12.

43   Michel de Certeau, *The Practice of Everyday Life,* trans. Steven Rendall (London: University of California Press, 2002). p. 117.

44 Elizabeth Grosz, 'BODIES- CITIES', in *Space, Time, and Perversion: Essays on the Politics of Bodies* (London: Routledge, 1995). p. 105.

45 The method of site sampling looks to incorporate the context of the author's surroundings. In the case of Harryman this is Detroit and this text looks to include the process of writing text, live conversations, versions of the live, Harryman's surroundings. Site Sampling is a process of capturing a site's text and I believe it offers a way of trapping, re-working and dismantling a site through text.

46 Carla Harryman, "Site Sampling In 'Performing Objects Stationed in the Sub World', in *Additional Apparitions*, ed. David Kennedy and Keith Tuma (Sheffield: Cherry On The Top Press, 2002). p.160.

47 Harryman, (2002). p.160.

48 Nick Kaye, *Site Specific Art: Performance, Place and Documentation* (London: Routledge, 2000). p. 39.

49 Elizabeth Grosz, 'Introduction', in *Space, Time, and Perversion: Essays on the Politics of Bodies*, (London: Routledge, 1995). p. 84.

50 Elizabeth Grosz, 'BODIES- CITIES', in *Space, Time, and Perversion* (1995). p. 105.

51 Kaye, (2000). p. 104.

52 *Ibid.,* p. 105.

53 Harryman, (2002). p. 166.

54 Redell Olsen, 'Sites And (Human) Non-Sites of A (Sub) Urban World' in *Additional Apparitions*, ed. David Kennedy and Keith Tuma (Sheffield: Cherry On The Top Press, 2002) p. 181

55 Harryman, (2002). p. 161

56 Harryman, (2002). p. 161

57 The Dreaming City: Glasgow 2020 and the Power of Mass Imagination, Demos.

58 Michel de Certeau, *The Practice of Everyday Life*, trans. Steven

Rendall (Berkley: University of California Press, 1988) p.117.

59 Further information about Linda France's work is available at: www.lindafrance.co.uk.

60 Interview conducted March 2007.

61 Further information about Aoife Mannix's work is available at: www.aoifemannix.com.

62 These can be downloaded from www.urbanwords.org .uk/urbanwords.

63 The whole project is documented on the project blog: www.almostanisland.blogspot.com.

64 Chris's article is available on the *A Place For Words* website: www.urbanwords.org.uk/aplaceforwords.

65 Text exhibited at Barking: A Model Town Centre, Barking Learning Centre, Autumn 2007

66 Liza Fior, of *muf Architecture/Art* sent me this in an email exchange, October 2008

67 Michel de Certeau, *The Practice of Everyday Life,* trans. Steven Rendall (Berkley: University of California Press, 1988). pp. 115-30.

68 This story can be downloaded from my website: www.sarahbutler.org.uk.

69 You can find out more about my work at www.urban-words.org.uk. www.shapingplace.ning.com is an online forum, hosted by UrbanWords, which encourages discussion about writing and place. Please also take a look at the *A Place For Words* website, which discusses the role of writing and Regeneration and has a wealth of case studies and downloadable articles: www.urbanwords.org.uk/a place forwords.

70 *2 Ennerdale Drive: unauthorised biography,* forthcoming 2011, Zero Books

71 Gaston Bachelard, *The Poetics of Space,* (Boston, Mass.: Beacon Press, 1994) p.8

72   Open discussion, Architexture conference, University of Strathclyde, April 2008

73   Rosi Braidotti, 'Nomadic Subjects: Embodiment and Difference', in *Contemporary Feminist Theory* (New York: Columbia University Press, 1994). p.54

74   Generally, Jane Rendell, *Art and Architecture: A Place Between* (London and New York: IB Tauris, 2006); and 'Invisible City' lecture, Institute of Germanic and Romance Languages, University of London, 7 May 2007

75   Esther Leslie, 'Telescoping the Microscopic Object: Benjamin the Collector' in *The Optic of Walter Benjamin*, edited by Alex Coles (London: Black Dog, 1998). p.63

76   Bachelard, p.8

77   Lynsey Hanley, *Estates: An Intimate History* (London: Granta Books, 2007).

78   Henri Lefebvre, *The Production of Space*, trans. Donald Nicholson-Smith (Oxford: Blackwell, 2009). pp. 38-9. Nicolson-Smith translates 'les *espaces de représentations*' as '*representational spaces*'; the translation I favour in this essay is derived from Andrew Merrifield's *Henri Lefebvre: A Critical Introduction* (New York and London: Routledge, 2006). I have chosen Merrifield's translation over Nicholson-Smith's not necessarily because it is more accurate but rather that I think it minimises confusion between the two terms.

79   This was the name of the school when it opened. However, by the time it was demolished, the name had been changed to Bettws High School, Bettws being the name of the council estate where the school was built.

80   James Stevens Curl, 'Brutalism', in *A Dictionary of Architecture and Landscape Architecture* (2000). Available at: http://www.encyclopedia.com [accessed 15 Mar. 2010]

81   Alison & Peter Smithson, *Without Rhetoric: An Architectural Aesthetic 1955–1972* (London: Latimer New Directions, 1973), p.6.

82   Reyner Bamham, *The New Brutalism* (London: The Architectural Press, 1966), pp. 46-7.

83   Eldred Evans and David Shalev are perhaps now best known for the Tate St Ives, Cornwall. Other buildings of theirs include: Jesus College building, Cambridge and Compton Verney Opera House, Warwickshire. More information about Evans and Shalev is available at: *www.evansandshalev.com*.

84   There is, as far as I know, no other school called 'The Sausage Factory', but interestingly a propaganda film, *Living at Thamesmead*, made for the GLC to encourage people to move to the new estate contains this exchange: 'At one point the boy looks over to the school and exclaims "it looks like a factory!" and the girl replies "better than my old one. *Old* was the word for it!"' Owen Hatherley, *Militant Modernism* (Winchester: Zero Books, 2008), pp. 38-9.

85   Arnulf Kolsted, 'What Happens if Zeleste Becomes an Architect?', in *Aesthetics, Well-being and Health: Essays within architecture and environmental aesthetics*, ed. Birgit Cold (Aldershot: Ashgate Publishers, 2001), p. 128.

86   For example, Lynsey Hanley (in reference to much municipal housing) laments bluntly: 'And concrete. Ugly concrete.' Lynsey Hanley, *Estates: An Intimate History* (London: Granta, 2007), p. 98.

87   Kolsted, p. 123.

88   Opposition to this tendency can be found in the writings of the Vorticist Wyndham Lewis, for whom a dependence 'on the collective sensibility of the period' made architecture 'the weakest of the arts'. Lewis wrote that 'if the world would only build temples to machinery in the abstract then everything would be perfect.' Wyndham Lewis quoted in Hatherley, pp. 27-8.

89   Kolsted, p. 126. One attempt in architecture (rather than literature) at tackling this situation is the 'User Participation

Process' that 'allows for the wants and needs of the users to be included in the final built environment'. This method was used successfully in the building of Hirstshals school in Denmark. As part of this process not only teachers but also the pupils themselves were asked to put forward their wishes and ideas. The architect then analysed all this input before designing the building. Consequently, the children showed more care for an environment they helped to create and 'vandalism and destruction [...] virtually disappeared'. It is perhaps interesting to note that '[t]he children felt a very strong need for a variety of spaces in the school, such as quiet spaces, noisy spaces, or soft spaces. [...] They also had specific wishes for colour: the youngest children selected the primary colours; older children introduced cooler colours'. Aase Eriksen, 'Creating Built Environments through the User Participation Process', *Aesthetics, Well-being and Health*, pp. 106-8.

90   However, it must be noted that Brutalist buildings are far from universally maligned. The Barbican in London, for instance, has many admirers and is at the time of writing a very fashionable (and expensive) place to live. See Jonathan Glancey, 'A great place to live'. Available at: http://www.guardian.co.uk/education/2001/sep/07/arts.high ereducation [accessed 5/7/2010]. One interesting champion of Brutalism (and its cultural significance in Britain) is the writer, Owen Hatherley, who argues that Brutalism is an 'architecture both of austerity *and* abundance, in line with the contradictions of the post-1945 melange of Socialism and Capitalism [...] accentuating the most fertile features of both'. For Hatherley, Brutalism is both 'Trotskyist' (as opposed to Stalinist) and 'glamorous' in its attempts to re-imagine sites as 'Pop Utopia[s]'. And although he uses words like 'inhuman' to describe the architecture, for him '[t]he only serious signs of Britain's continued cultural life

have been clearly brutalist-indebted' (such as hardcore, jungle and grime music). And even in a 'ruinous condition', these buildings, Hatherley would argue, 'can still offer a sense of possibility which decades of being told 'There is No Alternative' has almost beaten out of us.' Hatherley, pp. 3-42.

91   The Smithsons saw Brutalism as 'building for the socialist dream, which is something different from simply complying with a programme written by the socialist state' (The Smithsons in Hatherley, p. 33), and were concerned with what they perceived as the needs of communities. They were interested, for instance, in creating buildings that would 'promote the social associations that they had encountered in the social-anthropological work of Peter Willmot and Michael Young', and Nicholas Bullock argues that the 'Brutalist, no-nonsense aesthetic' of the Smithsons' Golden Lane project was 'intended to convey the gritty reality of working-class life'(Nicholas Bullock, 'Building the Socialist Dream or Housing the Socialist State? Design versus the Production of Housing in the 1960s', in *Neo-avant-garde and Postmodern: Postwar Architecture in Britain and Beyond*, ed. Mark Crinson and Claire Zimmerman (New Haven & London: Yale University Press, 2010), pp. 325-7). However, Brutalist buildings were still *representations of space* that were imposed from above, with little or no consultation with those who would actually inhabit or use them. I am unaware of any Brutalist architects using anything akin to the User Participation Process (mentioned above) in the construction of their buildings.

92   Lefebvre, p. 41.

93   Lefebvre, p. 42.

94   Quoted by Charles Olson in 'Projective Verse', *Postmodern American Poetry*, ed. Paul Hoover (New York: Norton, 1994), p. 614.

95 Jon Wright, 'Case Reports > Newport High School'. Available at: http://www.c20society.org.uk/casework/reports/2008/newport-high-school.html [accessed 8/6/2010]

96 Hatherley, p. 32.

97 Michael Davidson, 'Introduction', in George Oppen, *New Collected Poems* (New York: New Directions, 2008), p. xxxi.

98 Davidson, 'Notes', in Oppen, p. 378.

99 George Oppen, 'Of Being Numerous', in *New Collected Poems*, p. 165.

100 Oppen, p. 166.

101 Joan Retallack, *The Poethical Wager* (Berkeley and Los Angeles: University of California Press, 2002), p. 44.

102 Cynthia Hogue and Rebecca Ross, *When the Water Came: Evacuees of Hurricane Katrina (Interview-poems and photographs)*, forthcoming from UNO Press. A version of the work was showcased at *Skylines*, Centre for Contemporary Art and the Natural World, CCANW, Devon, June 2009 - an ecopoetics project I curated, details online at: http://www.theattendingfield.com.

103 Waldman spoke about this "outrageous metaphor" at the Study Abroad at the Bowery programme, Bowery Poetry Club, New York, August 2005; and Jena Osman reports a similar use of the term by Waldman at the Kelly Writers House, Philadelphia in, Jena Osman, "Is Poetry the News?: Poethics of the Found Text", *Jacket*, 32, 2007.

104 Anne Waldman, *Outrider* (Albuquerque: La Alameda Press, 2006).

105 Waldman, pp. 42-3.

106 Waldman, p. 43.

107 *Portrait of James Davidson* by Rebecca Ross, "James Davidson" interview-poem by Cynthia Hogue, from *When the Water Came: Evacuees of Hurricane Katrina*. Image used by permission, UNO Press 2010, ISBN 978-1-60801-012-7.

108 Waldman, pp. 79-80.

109 Waldman, p. 60.

110 Waldman, p. 47.

111 Waldman, pp. 60-1.

112 Waldman, p. 48.

113 Jena Osman, "Is Poetry the News?: Poethics of the Found Text", *Jacket*, 32, 2007.

114 Redell Olsen, *Secure Portable Space*. Hastings: Reality Street Editions, 2004.

115 Image from Jena Osman, "Is Poetry the News?: Poethics of the Found Text", *Jacket*, 32, 2007.

116 Extract from *Era of Heroes* taken from Redell Olsen, *Secure Portable Space* (Hastings: Reality Street, 2004), p.66. The font is an approximation of the one used in the book.

117 Retallack, p. 44.

118 "Victoria Green," from *When the Water Came: Evacuees of Hurricane Katrina*: 9-17; 26-27.

119 Retallack, p. 44.

120 A fuller view of the installation/intervention and other articles about it can be seen at the online catalogue: www.lyrik-installation.dk/Vaerloese. There is also a printed catalogue available.

121 William Blake, *The Marriage of Heaven and Hell*, in *William Blake: The Complete Illuminated Books*; introduction by David Bindman (London: Thames and Hudson, 2000)., p. 120, plate 14, ll. 17- 21.

122 William Blake, *Milton a Poem*, in *The Complete Illuminated Books* , p. 261, plate 14, ll. 21-27.

123 It is here essential to note that the real world for Blake is the World of Imaginations, the three dimensional Newtonian space or the two dimensional paper is a part of the Vegetative Illusion. Blake's form for antirealism corresponds well to postmodern theories of perceiving everything as text, as signs with infinite possibilities of reading. Though there is a very important difference in ontology. In

Blake's art everything has a complex existence in itself and in dialogue with others. In Blake's cosmos everything is animated, everything is humanized. See William Blake, *The Complete Poetry and Prose of William Blake;* Electronic Edition. ed. David V. Erdman. Commentary by Harold Bloom, Morris Eaves, Robert Essik, Joseph Viscomi. (Virginia: Institute for Advanced Technology in Humanities, 2001)., pp. 52651, pp. 552-4, pp. 554-60, pp. 95-144, pp. 663-4. Available at: www.blakearchive.org.

124 Nicoletta Isar, 'Vision and Performance | A Hierotopic Approach to Contemporary Art', in *Hierotopy Comparative Studies,* ed. A. Lidov (Moscow : Indrik, 2009).

125 Ninjalicious, *Access All Areas: A User's Guide to the Art of Urban Exploration* (Toronto: Infilpress, 2005), p. 4.

126 Steve Pile 'Memory and the City', in *Temporalities: Autobiography and Everyday Life.* ed. Jan Campbell and Janet Harbord (Manchester: Manchester University Press, 2002), p. 112.

127 Michel de Certeau, *The Practice of Everyday Life.* trans. Steven F. Randall (Berkeley and London: University of California Press, 1984), p. 117.

128 Henri Lefebvre, *Writings on Cities,* trans. and ed. Eleonore Kofman and Elizabeth Lebas (Cambridge, Massachusetts: Blackwell, 1996), p. 101.

129 Henri Lefebvre, *The Production of Space,* trans. Donald Nicholson-Smith (Oxford: Blackwell, 1991), p. 90.

130 Lefebvre (1991), p. 26.

131 Lefebvre (1991), p. 70.

132 Lefebvre (1991), p. 31.

133 Karen A Franck Quentin Stevens ,'Tying Down Loose Space,' in *Loose Space: Possibility and Diversity in Urban Life.* ed. Karen A Franck Quentin Stevens. (Oxford: Routledge, 2005). pp.10-11.

134 Not to be confused with the scholar and postmodern critic,

Nicholas Royle, based at the University of Sussex.

135 Nicholas Royle, in interview with David Kendall, *The Edge Magazine*, 2007. Available at: http://www.theedge.abel gratis.co.uk/royleiview.htm [accessed March 23, 2010]

136 Royle, in Kendall, 1997.

137 Nicholas Royle, *Counterparts* (London: Penguin, 1993) pp. 70-75.

138 Nicholas Royle, *The Matter of the Heart* (London: Abacus , 1997) . p. 20.

139 Royle (1997), p.83.

140 Royale (1997), p.141.

141 Royle (1997), p.164.

142 Royle (1997), p. 291.

143 Royle (1997), p.224.

144 Hayden Lorimer, 'Cultural geography: nonrepresentational conditions and concerns', in *Progress in Human Geography*, 32.4 (2008). p. 552.

145 Ben Anderson , 'Becoming and being hopeful: towards a theory of affect', in *Environment and Planning D: Society and Space*. 24.5 (2006). p. 738.

146 Nicholas Royle, *The Director's Cut* (London: Abacus, 2000). p. 89.

147 Royle (2000), p. 170.

148 Royle (2000), pp. 16-7.

149 Teresa Brennan, *The Transmission of Affect* (New York: Cornell University Press, 2004). p. 15.

150 Brennan (2004), p. 1.

151 Royle (2000), p. 277.

152 Brennan (2004), p. 12.

153 Royle, in Kendall, 2007.

154 Tim Edensor, *Industrial Ruins* (Oxford: Berg, 2005). p. 69.

155 Edensor (2005), p. 67.

156 Rebecca Solnit, *A Field Guide to Getting Lost* (New York and London: Penguin, 2006). p. 90.

157 Lazlo Moholy-Nagy, assisted by Cyril Jenkins and Hazen Sise, Museum of Modern Art Film Library.

158 Peder Anker, 'The Bauhaus of Nature', *Modernism/ Modernity*, Vol.12, No.2, p-.239.

159 Berthold Lubetkin, Notes for 'Samizdat', p.40. RIBA, Lubetkin's Papers, Box 1, LuB/25/4.

160 Jacques Derrida, *The Animal That Therefore I Am*. Ed. Marie-Louise Mallet. Trans. David Wills. (Fordham University Press, New York, 2007).

161 See the filmography at www.gorillamen.com.

162 Diana Fox Jones, "My Daddy was a Gorilla". This memoir has been brought together with other material relating to Charlie Gemora and the other Gorilla-Men of Hollywood at the excellent www.gorillamen.com.

163 Lubetkin, unpublished transcript, 'Dudley Zoo", c.1938. RIBA, Lubetkin's Papers, Box 1, LuB/25/4.

164 Lubetkin: in conversation 1974. Quoted in John Allan, *Berthold Lubetkin: Architecture and the Tradition of Progress* (London: RIBA Publications, 1992), p.208

165 Wyndham Lewis, "The Enemy of the Stars", *Collected Poems and Plays*, ed. Alan Munton (Carcanet: Manchester, 1979), p.95

166 "Mennonites trace their roots to Switzerland in the early sixteenth century, when a small group of reformers became known as "Anabaptists" or rebaptizers. They resisted not only the Catholic church but also reformers such as Calvin and Zwingli who sought to create a new state church in place of the old. Emphasizing believers' baptism, nonresistance, separation of church and state, and voluntary community, the Anabaptists found themselves vigorously persecuted as a threat to church and civil authority, but the movement gained small groups of adherents across Europe, especially in Switzerland, south Germany, and Holland. Some became known as Mennonites after the Dutch church leader and former priest Menno Simons. The Amish split

from the less conservative groups in a 1693 schism, but close contacts continued. Large numbers of Mennonites began to emigrate to North America in the seventeenth century, and many Amish followed. Passage among groups, especially from Amish to Mennonite, as continued. Today over half of the million-plus Mennonites worldwide are in South Africa, Africa, and Asia, with about 450,000 in Canada and the United States." Quoted from Jeff Gundy "New Maps of the Territories: On Mennonite Writing" in The Georgia Review, 11.4. Pg. 871.

167 Di Brandt, *So this is the world & here I am in it* (Edmonton: NeWest Press, 2007, p.1)

168 Donna Bailey Nurse, 'Di Brandt: Poems of passionate accusation' , in *Quill & Quire 70:6*, pp. 1.

169 Di Brandt, *Now You Care* (Toronto: Coach House Books, 2003, p. 13-14.)

170 Di Brandt, qtd. in Jeff Gundy's 'New Maps of the Territories: On Mennonite Writing' in *The Georgia Review LVII/4* (Winter 2003, pp. 877.)

171 Di Brandt, *Now You Care* (Toronto: Coach House Books, 2003, p.)

172 Di Brandt, *Now You Care* (Toronto: Coach House Books, 2003, p.).

173 Annette Kolodny, qtd. in Cheryl Lousley's 'Home on the Prairie? A Feminist and Postcolonial Reading of Sharon Butala, Di Brandt, and Joy Kogawa' in *Interdisciplinary Studies in Literature and Environment 8.2* (Summer 2001, pp. 71.)

174 Of Laguna, Sioux, Scottish, and Lebanese-American descent, Paula Gunn Allen (1939-2008) was born and raised in New Mexico. She received her Ph.D. from the University of New Mexico in 1975. Allen, a well-known feminist, received high praise for her creative writing, which promoted the richness of Native American culture.

Contemporary culture has eliminated both the concept of the public and the figure of the intellectual. Former public spaces – both physical and cultural – are now either derelict or colonized by advertising. A cretinous anti-intellectualism presides, cheerled by expensively educated hacks in the pay of multinational corporations who reassure their bored readers that there is no need to rouse themselves from their interpassive stupor. The informal censorship internalized and propagated by the cultural workers of late capitalism generates a banal conformity that the propaganda chiefs of Stalinism could only ever have dreamt of imposing. Zer0 Books knows that another kind of discourse – intellectual without being academic, popular without being populist – is not only possible: it is already flourishing, in the regions beyond the striplit malls of so-called mass media and the neurotically bureaucratic halls of the academy. Zer0 is committed to the idea of publishing as a making public of the intellectual. It is convinced that in the unthinking, blandly consensual culture in which we live, critical and engaged theoretical reflection is more important than ever before.